Contra Mundum Press

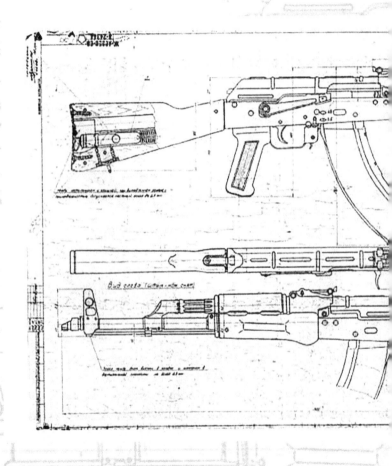

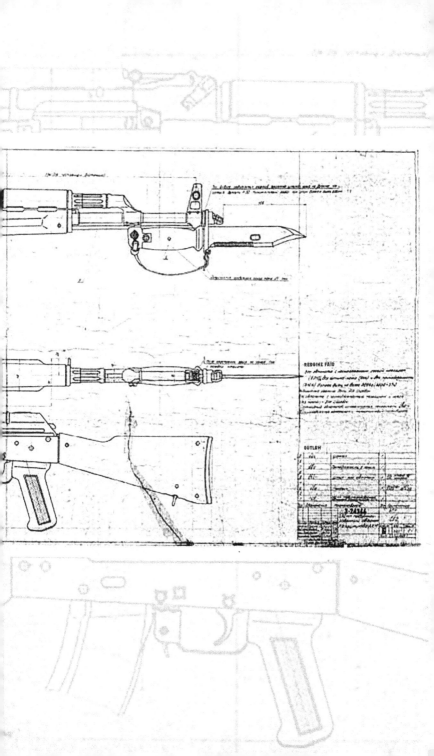

OUTLAW

Author Armed & Dangerous

RÉDOINE FAÏD

Interviews with Jérôme Pierrat

Translated by
John Galbraith Simmons
& Jocelyne Geneviève Barque

Contra Mundum Press   New York · London · Melbourne

Translation & preface © 2020 John Galbraith Simmons & Jocelyn Geneviève Barque; *Braqueur* © Mazarine / Librairie Arthème Fayard, 2016; postface © Jérôme Pierrat.

Library of Congress Cataloguing-in-Publication Data

Faïd, Rédoine, 1972 – ;
Pierrat, Jérôme, 1971–

[Braqueur: Des cités au grand banditisme. English.]
Outlaw: Author Armed & Dangerous / by Rédoine Faïd & Jérôme Pierrat; translated from the French by John Galbraith Simmons & Jocelyn Geneviève Barque

—1st Contra Mundum Press Edition
264 pp., 5 × 8 in.

ISBN 9781940625386

   I. Faïd, Rédoine ; Pierrat, Jérôme.
  II. Title.
 III. Simmons, John Galbraith & Barque, Jocelyn Geneviève.
 IV. Translators.
  V. Simmons, John Galbraith.
 VI. Preface.
VII. Pierrat, Jérôme.
VIII. Postface.

2020935362

PREFACE

"The Author," as Rédoine Faïd became known among fellow inmates in French penitentiaries, is a bank thief with executive talent and explosives expertise, a hostage taker who avoided physically harming his captives, and a serial prison escapee and recidivist. He is also a cinephile whose life and work lends a further dimension to Jean-Luc Godard's celebrated notion that cinema is truth at 24 frames per second.

Outlaw is at once a criminal autobiography and a prison memoir, comparable to such works as Paddy Mitchell's *This Bank Robber's Life* and Chester Himes' account of his career in *The Quality of Hurt & My Life of Absurdity*. This hybrid construction holds advantages for both Faïd's narrative and the wider meaning it conveys. By way of interview format with journalist Jérôme Pierrat, Faïd recounts his career from his youth as a delinquent in the housing projects outside Paris to his capture in 1998, in the wake of a series of sophisticated armed robberies, after which he was held in a clutch of French prisons, often in solitary confinement.

Although Faïd's narrative ends in 2009, the postface to this book summarizes his subsequent activity, which included release from prison, further spectacular heists, and three prison escapes. He was on the run as recently as July 1, 2018, after a dramatic helicopter breakout from a penitentiary near

Paris that made front-page news in France and the United States alike, and ended with his capture three months later.

For an American reader, Faïd's life and work has a certain congruence with a frame established by Willie Sutton (1901–1980), the career criminal who robbed banks not, as one reporter had it, "because that's where the money is," but because he enjoyed it. Sutton's historic significance is actually much greater and, in terms of the dynamics that shaped their *modus operandi* and accounts for their renown, he and Faïd share several striking traits. Like Sutton, Faïd proved to be a compulsive thief who graduated from petty crime to banks. He eventually focused on the armored truck, which presents a greater challenge to rob. Also like Sutton, his interest in money was quite secondary to the excitement and adrenaline rush of the heist. Each man operated with careful plans; and Faïd, like Sutton, cultivated an easy relationship with organized crime, in prison and out. In addition, both avoided inflicting physical violence on victims, and they claimed that the pistol or machine gun was basically a prop. Finally, Sutton and Faïd each embarked on multiple & carefully planned prison escapes, some of them spectacular.

For all the various differences in legal vocabulary, *Outlaw* comes readily into English and offers a novel take on the genre of "true crime." In all memoirs, and especially criminal autobiographies, the author is in some measure a selective and unreliable narrator. Faïd is no exception. However, he reveals larger truths behind journalistic perspectives that are restricted to accommodating social norms and, often enough, moralistic preconceptions. Most notable is Faïd's education by way of films such as *Thief* and *Scarface* and especially Michael Mann's *Heat*. His career demonstrates the way in which cinematic experience abridges, as often as it seals, the social contract. Faïd's nickname among his accomplices was "Doc," after Steve McQueen's portrayal of the determined and intelligent hero in *The Getaway*, a film by Sam Peckinpah after a novel by noir icon Jim Thompson.

Similarly, the fact that Faïd and his accomplices concentrated on armored vehicles testifies mainly to advances in bank security and efforts to keep money safe from people like him. Faïd judged brick and mortar banks risky by comparison with the exciting task of immobilizing and blasting open a vault on wheels to confront a couple of guards, who would tend to comply when faced with a rocket launcher, submachine guns, and men wearing Halloween masks.

Karl Marx once archly asked if the Tree of Sin were not identical to the Tree of Knowledge. "And would locks," he wondered, "ever have reached their present degree of excellence had there been no thieves?" That was 150 years ago. Today Rédoine Faïd is able to tell you, by way of *Outlaw*, in entertaining and expert detail, that the answers to these questions are clear: yes *&* no.

— John Galbraith Simmons

OUTLAW

Author Armed & Dangerous

Little Brother got a wish to be a big man
That's why he played tough since he was 10
Taught by TV news, as he's growin' up
Guys don't do what he say, he beats 'em to a pulp
Age 13, he's mad for cash
Little Brother matures, but much too fast
Dreamin' of hot rods, clothes, and bread
He don't give a damn what tomorrow says
Little Brother whacks his toy soldiers to go to war
Thinkin' 'bout the loot he was gonna score

Akhenaton *&* IAM

For Kamel Hérizi, whom I regarded as my brother.
For Rallyan, Anissa, and Hermès, whom I greatly esteem.
For my mother, who died too young.
For my father, from whom I ask forgiveness.

France-Soir

June 9, 1997

Essonne. *During the robbery, not a single shot was fired. Using a dump truck to crash into an armored truck, the gangsters grabbed the money & ran.*

A quick heist, like stealing candy from a baby, near suburban Fleury-Mérogis. A lucrative payday for skilled members of a gang that sped off, thumbing their noses at the police. Speed, teamwork, and organization: if armed robbery was an honorable profession, workers like these would be some of the best in France. [...]

It was 6 PM Saturday on Route 31. The armored truck ACDS 2460 was quietly speeding toward Vert-le-Grand, south of Bondoufle. Inside, three security guards were looking forward to a relaxing weekend. End of their shift in sight, no reason to worry.

But they didn't know that, coming into Montaubert, they were entering the jaws of a well-laid trap. Cars positioned on both sides of the highway slowed traffic at two roundabouts. The dump truck advances. It plowed head-on into the armored vehicle. A titanic shock at 50 MPH. No time to count the wounds or check the bruises. The thieves would help themselves. As the armored truck lay in a ditch, a second team of commandos in a white Peugeot 405 screeched to a halt at the scene. Armed and wearing balaclavas, they took an axe to the windshield. No gunfire.

They forced open the doors. In no time, having emptied the truck of its treasure, they made their getaway in three cars. True to the image of professionals who keep their powder dry, time was really money. The heist went down inside of five minutes.

Why have you decided to tell your story?

At first, I wasn't crazy about the idea. What's past is buried and should stay that way. Even though I don't have blood on my hands, I'm not proud of what I've done. But now, with the inner cities and the projects always in the news, you've convinced me that my life might show why kids from the projects get tangled up in delinquency. I don't want to justify myself. But I do want to take down some of the stereotypes that never seem to go away.

You've just come out of prison. What had you done and how long were you behind bars?

What I did was enough to get the police special forces and the national gendarmerie on my case. I was arrested the 30ᵗʰ of December 1998 at age 26. I spent New Year's Eve in custody at Fresnes Penitentiary under high security. I was later sentenced to 19 years for armed robberies: banks, jewelry stores, armored trucks. Jailbreak, too. I was released in spring 2009. After close to 10 years in prison! A quarter of my life…

In fact, your story is that of a small-time thief who turns into a gangster, like many kids from the projects who grow up in the shadow of the criminal milieu, yet outside it.

That's right. I'm self-taught. I was never caught for petty theft or neighborhood robberies. Unfortunately that led to bigger crimes. I took some care to avoid total chaos. But I made bad choices and you pay for that.

We're not going to do a *Garde à vue* style interrogation.[*] So, introduce yourself.

My family comes from a small village in the high-lands in Algeria, about 125 miles south of Algiers. My father was a peasant like his father before him, but he was also a hunter's guide. That made him a valu-able recruit for the Algerian Resistance; he knew every little path in the region and was an excellent marksman. After he and his comrades launched a surprise attack against French soldiers to steal guns, he was ratted out. As payback, his village was burned down. But my family wasn't hurt. Local police who were escorts for the military protected my mother, sisters, & brothers. So my father owed the Algerian police eternal gratitude. Before the war, they used to hunt with my father and they liked him.

Months after this incident, he was caught, put in jail, and tortured. He was saved by a visit from the International Red Cross, which intervened to have him hospitalized. After which he was quietly released and he recovered in the home of a sympa-thizer, where he stayed until the end of the war. A year later he returned to France to get back his old job in a chemical factory, the Kuhlmann Factory in Villers-Saint-Paul in the Oise. Why did he emigrate in 1950, then find himself in Algeria during the war,

---

[*] The narrative frame of *Garde à vue* (*The Inquisitor*), a 1981 French crime film directed by Claude Miller, is a police interro-gation. It is based on the novel *Brainwash* by John Wainwright.

yet return to France? That's a long story to come back to... But it's how my sisters and brothers were born in Algeria whereas I was born in Creil. In 1969, my father was rejoined by his family.

How did that come about?

The office of social services at the factory made it possible. Every year he'd been taking a month or two of unpaid leave to visit Algeria. So now he could bring over his wife and seven children to offer them a better future than they would've had in a village devastated by the war and offering no means of subsistence. In France, my parents had three more kids, including me, born in May 1972. So I'm the next to last of 10 children. We lived at the time in a small three-bedroom apartment in Plateau Rouher, one of four housing projects in the heights above Creil. In 1975, we moved to a new place on rue Guynemer. That was where I grew up. We lived in a large apartment, about 1500 square feet.

What was it like at home?

Despite his night job at the factory, my father took care of me. Nights at 8 PM he got on his little Moby-lette scooter with his lunch pail and left for work. An hour after he got home at 6:00 in the morning, he woke me up and made my breakfast. Then he took me to school, and came back again to take me home for lunch. From my childhood in the 1970s, two memories stand out.

The first is from when I was five years old and in kindergarten. It was a Friday, after my parents returned from shopping. It must have been 4 o'clock. I was still in nursery school, which ended at 4:20. The schoolyard gate was three feet high with bars and I could see outside. I was there with my little brother, Nordine, who was sickly and an epileptic. So we see our parents parking in front of the school and call to them. Smiling, my father sees me and crosses the street. The school was just a little ways from the building where we lived. My brother was crying and didn't want to be there. So my father tells him, "Hang on, we're taking you home. Don't cry." He takes hold of Nordine and pulls him up over the bars.

—And what about me, Papa?

—You, you're not crying. You're a big guy.

Strange, but I feel sure that that little incident made me who I am. It made me tougher. My hands clenching the bars, I watched my parents leave and swallowed my anger.

The second memory is from 1979. Jacques Mesrine* was executed at Porte de Clignancourt. His death was announced on television. My whole family was sad. For us, Mesrine stood for the people against the rich and powerful. Damn! They killed him! We talked about it at home. Everybody said that he was a good man, an intelligent guy. Through the 1980s, not one year went by that we didn't talk about Mesrine. He stayed with me.

---

* A charismatic and celebrated criminal, Mesrine (1936–1979) was sometimes likened to Robin Hood.

There was no delinquency in your family?

None. They were all honest people. My brother Abdeslam obtained his bac C.* Leila, my sister, went to law school. My brothers Rachid and Djamel worked their whole lives. Abderrahmane, my other brother, studied in Iraq and now lives in Algeria, where he teaches math at the university. My brother Fayçal, two years older than me, studied law at the university.

As for me, I didn't like school, though I was a pretty good student. But disruptive. I got bored. I started to play hooky. In primary school, Fayçal and I used to hang out at the mall in Creil. In fact, that's where I stole for the first time.

How old were you?

I was 6 and my brother 8. It was a time when shopping centers were popping up everywhere. For us it was Disneyland. There was all this candy and toys and stuff that we who lived in the projects could only look at but other kids could buy. Creil is surrounded by wealthy suburbs like Chantilly and Senlis. Even people who lived in downtown Creil had money enough. It wasn't right, I said to myself from the beginning. We were just like them.

The store had no cameras and only one security guard. He called us "petit merguez." We didn't mind; we were Arabs. We put up with it, although at home it was taboo and something we never talked about.

* Bac C, for students in physics and math, was considered at the time (1968–1994) the most prestigious baccalaureate degree.

I don't remember how the idea came to me, but at all events we set about helping ourselves.

At the time, the shopping center was located across a big cornfield. We used to pick corn and peel it, but soon found it disgusting. So we'd leave our school bags in the field and go mess around in the shopping center.

We'd go back and forth through the aisles and fill up a shopping basket with candies, cookies, toys, miniature cars, comic books, etc. At the time, a small fortune. You could walk right out. It was crazy.

The security guard paid no attention, we were only kids. We left the store, turned around to check, but everything was fine. We crossed the parking lot and once in the cornfield, we shared the booty. It worked fine until the day we got a plastic bag from the fruits and vegetable department and filled it up with miniature cars. We were just novices and a sales clerk who knew us from the neighborhood pointed us out. The security guard nabbed us. My brother took them to our stash. When the guard saw all that we'd stolen, he went nuts and called our parents. When my mother arrived we'd just been let go and ran off. She called the school and found out we'd been truant for three weeks. With everything we were stealing, we'd stopped wanting to show up at school.

That night my parents looked for us everywhere. My brother Fayçal was hiding in the stairway and I was in the basement. A girl living in the building finally convinced me to go back home. I was afraid my father was going to beat me. If there was one thing he abhorred, it was theft. And, in fact, he took us in the bathroom once we got back, removed his belt, and gave us each 20 lashes. He was furious. As somebody who worked hard, made sacrifices, he was really shocked. My mother asked me why we'd do such a thing. She'd paid the store for what we'd stolen. I thanked her and promised never to do it again.

My father forgave us, too, thinking it was just the kind of stupid thing that kids do.

So because you lied to your mother, we're talking today.

When school started the next year I was in CE1,* I began stealing money out of the wallets of my sisters and brothers to buy pastries. I got caught and slapped. But I told myself that was to be expected. The next year I spent time in the library, reading comics & running around with rich kids, which gave me new ideas.

With three friends from the neighborhood — an African, a Chinese, and an Antillean — we formed quite a cosmopolitan gang. We started stealing. It was exactly like the scene in *Sleepers* with Robert De Niro: a kid steals some little thing from a store, the owner chases him while his friends clean out the place. Sometimes my father beat me and I ended up repeating CE2. Money was what I wanted. When I turned 11, there were other needs: 501 jeans, Adidas Natase sneakers, Tachini track suits!

---

* The first grade, for children 6–7 years old.

One thing I did plunged me straight into being a delinquent. We were invited to a party in Creil put on by some bourgeois girls. They rented a neighborhood discotheque, Le Lido, on a Wednesday afternoon. Inside were only lily-white French kids, sons of upper-class families. And beautiful nice girls, or so I thought, anyway. I had my first kiss with one of them and stayed with her for a month and a half.

This was the era of Hip-hop and Sidney, "Let's Break (Smurf)," Michael Jackson, funk bands. We danced and ate and drank as much as we wanted. After that, are we going back home? No way, 'bro — no fucking way! Meanwhile one of us found out that to pay for the party, one of the little rich girls had burglarized an apartment! She stole the keys from a friend, and lifted the television & a video recorder, which she sold for 2,000 francs. So then, I thought — *that's wild*. It knocked me out. You can't tell me that, it would've been better if I didn't know. It makes me figure, in fact, that what you can't get legally, you've got to take.

It was like a slap in the face. Things have got to change. There were basement rooms where we lived, on rue Guynemer. We decided we'd make our own discotheque. We laid carpet on the floor, put up posters, all that stuff. And then we robbed this fucking nursery school.

Bravo for that!

Right. Well, we stole the hotplate and the record player. When everything was ready, one guy who was in middle school brought over all his girlfriends. We were stars. But then the problem was we needed drinks and stuff to eat. So we decided to target apartments, steal televisions and sell them. And we shoplifted from supermarkets. By now, as delinquents, we had five years' experience. One or two guys would make it seem like they were stealing. They distracted security while we went to plunder. And we got better at stealing. We'd tape windows before breaking them — that kind of thing. We made sure not to get caught. We started to dress sharp and take our girls to the movies. All this while still going to school. I was 12 and knew stealing was going to be my profession.

We kept robbing supermarkets and apartments until I was about 15. We must have done about 80, all told. We even had fences to buy the televisions, stereo systems, and other stuff. For example, a VHS brought 1500 francs. For five minutes' work. Compare that with what you'd earn from little jobs. You didn't think twice.

Which is to say — what exactly?

After unloading food at the market from 4 to 8 in the morning, I'd go back at 11 and work until 2 in the afternoon. Eight hours working like a dog, I'd make 200 francs. With my buddies, we'd pick daffodils and lilies of the valley behind the Cora shopping center and sell bouquets for two francs a piece. We'd clean windshields in the Auchan parking lot. Problem was, ten of us had to split the money so we ended up with only 30 or 40 francs each compared to 1500 francs for a video recorder. That made it an easy choice. The logic is not great but it's inescapable. On top of which, we knew that the kids who lived in downtown Creil didn't need to work. They played soccer and went to the movies with money their parents gave them.

So you started to have money?

The trouble with theft is that after a while you don't want to steal your clothes. You want money to pay for them. That's not the same thing. You take the next step when you start thinking like that, convinced you've got to have a nice wad of cash. In *Scarface,* Tony Montana talks with his partner Manolo. They're sitting at a table and in his Cuban accent Tony says:

— Here it's like paradise. In five years I'll be billionaire, I'll have a Cadillac and a lotta dough. This town is like a big hairy pussy that's waiting to get fucked.

Then they get up from the table and we see they're dressed to the nines: pleated slacks, fancy shirts, loafers. And what's more, they're carrying shopping bags: they haven't stolen anything. They've just been shopping. A little while ago they were selling hot dogs and working shit jobs.

For us, maybe we weren't getting billions, but we made out. We had 501 Levis in every style & Lacoste polo shirts in every color you could name.

What did your mother say, seeing you so well dressed?

My mother was seriously sick... and my father was never there during the week. In the early 80s, he'd decided to invest his savings in a butcher shop in Paris, in Barbès.* They kept the apartment on rue Guynemer but moved to rue Léon. I kept going to school in Creil but went home to the new place only on weekends. But that put the finishing touches on my education as a delinquent. Because Barbès is a paradise for every kind of petty thief and schemer.

Around the neighborhood, I met Stéphane and Bruno. They were feujs,† a couple of years older than me. They were poor. They'd followed the same chaotic path as me but Paris-style. They were more streetwise. For instance, they knew how to open an apartment door using a phone card. They would break into mailboxes and steal new American Express cards that they resold for 400 francs each. Soon I got as good as them. Car radios was their thing at the time. Bruno was a real ace. You had no shortage of fences in Barbès, so we kept doing it.

---

* A low-income neighborhood in the 18th arrondissement, with a large population of North Africans.

† Feuj, a verlan modification of Juif (Jew), is a slang word, sometimes derogatory, for Jewish.

Every night. With the money we copped, I discovered new stuff. Karate movies at Opéra, prostitutes who opened their arms to 13-year-olds like me... and a pair of Westons! Not to mention Paris itself, which I roamed throughout during school vacations.

In 1984, my father lost his butcher shop. He saw some of his competitors were selling meat bought in the market at Rungis like it was certified Halal. After he warned the faithful at the mosque on rue Myrrha, they got back at him by sending city health inspectors and tax people. In short, they caused him problems and he was forced to close.

Also, my mother wasn't any good at business. She had a good heart and would let people buy on credit. And at the end of three months, she'd wipe the ledger clean. A good example was Stéphane's mother, who'd need to buy meat for the Jewish holidays but didn't have enough money to buy kosher.

When it came to us, our two mothers were the ones to sound the alarm. They knew we were in trouble. They'd have coffee together and wonder what was going on with their boys.

After the butcher shop closed, my parents went back to rue Guynemer. There I was way ahead of the times with hocking car radios, and I made fistfuls of money. Stéphane and Bruno were happy to take the train out to join me in Creil, and I'd do the same to see them in Paris.

And then what did you do?

We soon decided to go into burglary, with what was happening circa 1985. It amounted to three simple letters: IBM. Computers. We jumped in with both feet, breaking into classrooms and businesses. At the time you had no infrared alarms, only motion detectors at the exits. We'd hide inside the factory or warehouse and just empty the place. We made a small fortune. A computer went for between 3000–5000 francs, a huge sum at the time. But you couldn't do that every day.

To step up the rhythm, we decided to get into computer warehouses. We located one in an industrial park near Compiègne. The place was like Ali Baba's cave but with security bars on the windows. On the advice of a fence, we bought a crowbar and went there at two in the morning. We twisted off the bars, taped the windows, broke them, and made a razzia of 40 items: printers, scanners, computers. Jackpot! The fence arrived with his truck. We passed the whole lot out through the back windows.

Our guy couldn't even take it all. He gave us the address of another fence near Bastille who accepted the rest but paid by check... To find somebody to cash it, I went around to all my friends and their sisters and cousins. In the end, the three of us came away with 60,000 francs. From that moment on, we never stopped committing burglaries.

Only computers?

No, all sorts of merchandise. Like this clothing store in Creil. It was equipped with sensors on the windows and doors, and there was an infrared burglar alarm. Going there to buy a sweater, I noticed that the storeroom butted up against the stairway in the neighboring building. With a screwdriver, a skeleton key from the fire department that I copped from a hospital nurse, and a phone card, we got into the stairway and went down to the storeroom. There the steel door was also equipped with a sensor. We got into the place *à la Spaggiari*.* Our friend, a fence who worked in construction, had given us a blowtorch and taught us how to use it. Next day at two in the morning, he parked his truck in the front of the store. We went downstairs and emptied the storeroom, putting everything in plastic garbage bags. Sweaters, polo shirts — everybody shopped at this place. We came away with 90,000 francs.

We kept it up with offices, perfume and tobacco stores, and sports bars. I can't even count how many nights I spent scratching Millionaire! We looted non-stop for two years.

---

* Professional thief Albert Spaggiari made headlines with an elaborate break-in at the Société Générale bank in Nice in 1976. His exploits are recounted in his books, *Faut pas rire avec les barbares* (1977), *Les égouts du paradis* (1978), and *Le journal d'une truffe* (1983). For two English translations, see *Fric-Frac: The Great Riviera Bank Robbery* (1979), and *The Sewers of Gold* (1981).

Guys who delivered video and electronics equipment asked us to rob them during their shifts: sound systems, cassette recorders, fridges, even hot plates! It was funny, we were like an electronics department store. It was like we had the whole catalogue for Darty. We were almost becoming salesmen.

The biggest fence in Plateau Rouher was Fat Nagui. He lived on the 9th floor of a big building in Cavée, Creil:

—I saw it at Darty. How much?

—Sells for five grand. You can have it for two and we'll even deliver.

One day, this young Moroccan from the Plateau asked me about business, if it was good.

—What are you talking about? Sure, it's good.

—So, when can you bring us in, too? What you're up to.

This guy was dealing hashish and observing us. He was part of the younger generation of shit sellers. They were fearless and seemed to think we were crackerjacks.

We knew it wouldn't be smart to brag. The only time we'd meet guys from other neighborhoods was at soccer matches or Sunday afternoons at Le Lido, the discotheque in lower Creil. That was how it worked in the projects. You had the stairwells, basements, and apartments to yourselves when your parents were gone. Other times, you were out screwing around. The story was the same for everybody.

What about the police?

At the time we were obviously concerned about cops, especially the BAC.* Older guys warned us because they'd already been arrested. We knew the police by name. They'd watched us growing up but didn't know what we were doing, didn't have the slightest idea. They were thrown off because each time they came by, we'd be playing soccer. They didn't see us hanging out with the older guys or even smoking cigarettes. We didn't drink alcohol or spend time with drug dealers.

It's unbelievable, but we never got caught. The only time I got busted was in 1991, when Sega Mega Drive came out. This guy told me, "If you bring me the games, I can resell them all." So I holed up with a buddy in a big department store that closed every day between noon and 2:00 PM. We ransacked the place: Montblanc fountain pens, CDs, VHS recorders... Coming out, we got nabbed. That was the first time I got taken in. I was 18. They had nothing on me. So they just took my name and I could go. Basta.

The second time was a check cashing scheme. A buddy knew a guy who worked in a bank and had this super scam: one of us would open an account and the guy would give him a checkbook that he'd report as stolen on a Friday afternoon at 5:00 PM. Right after, he'd send a written confirmation to the headquarters in Beauvais, which was closed on the weekend, so notification wouldn't occur until Monday. Meanwhile

* *Brigade Anti-Commando*, a gang intelligence unit.

we'd seriously go to town. One time I found a guy to open an account and get a checkbook with 40 checks. I bought a suit & tie, rented a car, and shopped like mad — Darty, Auchan, etc. At Weston's, I bought two pairs of shoes. At the time there was no limit on the number of checks you could write.

But then the guy with the checkbook decided to go shopping himself. And what did the asshole do? He went alone and filled up a shopping cart without checking the prices. Security thought that was strange. So as he was leaving, the guy got stopped. The guard was disappointed when he saw the ID card & checkbook were legit. But they suspected a scam. They didn't want to let him go. The shopping cart held stuff worth 8000 francs, a lot of money at the time.

So the guard made a copy of the checkbook and wrote down his license plate. Three days later the cops nabbed him. And the guy fingered me.

—You're screwed, said the cop who came to get me: He said it was you.

—I don't even know the guy.

I denied everything. They called the prosecutor, but this was not going to put me in jail. At court, I got a suspended sentence. But then le proc appealed and I got two months, mandatory. I pleaded my case without a lawyer. Finally the sentence was annulled. I told them that I was going to school and that they were going to destroy my life. It was at the Court of Appeals in Amiens.

Those were my two run-ins with the courts. After that they didn't see me again until December 30, 1998, when the national police got involved after the armored truck robbery...

Was there a lot of criminal activity in and around Creil?

None in the 1980s. There was no hashish. You had a little marijuana because of the Netherlands, but even that was relatively low-key. No cocaine or heroin. With delinquents, it was petty thievery, robbing stores and delivery trucks. Only Gauls, 18 years old, like friends of my brother Djamel, who'd done a month in jail.

I thought nobody in your family has a criminal record.

I'd forgotten. I was really young at the time. Djamel went away for a month because he was caught driving a Mobylette stolen by a neighborhood buddy. When he got out, he never screwed around again. Prison changed him; he was never the same.

At the time, jail either hardened you or broke you. The tough guys, Djamel's friends, were three years older than us. These fuckers stole from stores. Fish, pizzas, they didn't care. They'd go after stuff in Gel 2000!* Anything not nailed down, they'd rob it.

Christian, one of my brother's friends, was an ace burglar. He could run super-fast, a regular cheetah. He'd hide inside the walk-in freezer and at night load

---

* A specialty supermarket in France that sells frozen food.

up a shopping cart. He robbed apartments, stores, anything. One day he decided to move to Paris. But there the cops weren't the same. You had more patrols and plenty of plainclothes detectives. On top of which, in the 1980s, a lot of terrorism. One night, when a friend who was staying with him needed a fix, this guy played the hero and went out to score a couple of hits. The narcs caught him and after that were out to get him. They found out how to make him think with two years in Fresnes. When he came out, his mother was dead. He really worked on himself to change. He always urged me not to screw up, to stay out of jail. To scare me, he told me about Michel Lepage:*

—I was in Division 3 with him. He was known in the banlieue as a godfather. In prison, he could mix it up with a guard and nobody would bat an eye. This guy was a heavy.

And years later, in the penitentiary at Moulins, I met the famous gangster.

—First time I heard about you, I told him, was from a guy who'd just come out of Fresnes in 1983, when I was 11 years old. He wanted to scare me about going to jail. It had the opposite effect. Your story fascinated me. You became a star. Bank robber and prison escapee. I told myself: that's for me.

---

* A major figure in armed robbery in France beginning in the 1970s, Lepage was also known for a spectacular prison escape in 1977. His own autobiography, *Banlieue sud: Ma vie de gangster*, was published in 2011.

Tell me more about what was going down in the projects.

At the time, around 1984, we were skipping classes and hanging out in the stairwells, which were still clean. Nobody ate or smoked in them. But the next generation, in the 1990s, brought empty soda cans and joints all over the place that screwed up everything. You had trash & cigarette butts, and then all the stuff that hashish dragged in.

The drug business started about 1985. The first time I saw barrettes,* my brother Fayçal showed them to me. That was not my thing at all, never was. In fact, I detested it. One day a good buddy showed me what he was carrying in his sock: two packs of Marlboros filled up with 20 barrettes, each worth 100 francs. He was selling but I just walked away and never thought twice. It didn't interest me and I thought it could just get me in trouble.

How did that business develop?

At first, it was only barrettes. A couple of guys from the projects would go to Holland to buy 200-gram *savonnettes,* sometimes kilos. But most of the supply was from old Moroccan guys from the neighborhood who'd come back from vacation with 5 to 10 kilos. Workers smuggled the drug in the family Peugeot. But small-time dealers in Creil had a problem: they themselves were the main users. Of a kilo, they'd

---

* The prevalent form of hashish as sold in France, about 10 grams, or $\frac{1}{3}$ ounce.

smoke 700 grams. As soon as they got a little money, they bought polo shirts and slacks, Lacoste jackets and Stan Smith kicks. The usual attire. They were flashy for a couple of months but then were hanging around waiting for the next summer vacation.

At the same time you had more serious sellers, clever Moroccans who had been trafficking for years but stayed below the radar. These guys might bring back 500–800 kilos a year but they didn't sell it locally. By way of Creil, they sent it on to Holland. Looking at them, you'd never know. They were like ghosts, these Maghreb billionaires. They bought from cousins or brothers who had estates in Morocco.

I met one of these guys at the detention center at Meaux. Oueri was an Algerian who worked with the Moroccans. He was busted at La Courneuve in July 2004, with his truck loaded with four tons of high-quality *Sum* hashish — minus 420 kilos for the snitch, or so it was said. Oueri was a 50-year-old Algerian with no record. He spent four years inside, then died a year after he got out. The guy was such an unknown to the police that he managed not to give his real name for eight months in detention at Nanterre. Unfortunately for him, he confided in his cellmate, who ratted on him. The cops discovered he owned an estate in Brittany, houses and businesses and such. In short, he belonged to the powerful Algerian-Moroccan mafia. These people mostly kept to themselves but Oueri didn't mind working with a guy from the projects. Which is why he got into such a mess.

What about the big dealers in the projects?

They turned up in the late 1990s. But these guys didn't spend five years selling barrettes before going into the import side of the business. No, the generation after us went straight to the top.

When we lived at 3 rue Guynemer, there were three Maghreb families. Ours was one, then the Ferguouguis — none of whom was a delinquent even though they used to hang out with me and my friends — and a Moroccan family who moved in after us, with a son named Djamel. He was my next-door neighbor and ten years younger. Underneath his friendly exterior, you could already tell he'd go places. While still really young he had his own little gang, seven or eight kids... Among them was his cousin, Fat Mourad, who got caught on a *go fast*.* While still a minor, Djamel — now known as Mosquito — spent four years in jail for serious juvenile delinquency. After that first stretch, he stayed out for a couple of years, which gave him time to become the number-one *go-faster* in the Oise before being busted by José, a tough cop from the branch office in Creil.

Mosquito didn't realize what was happening. He thought he was dealing with local cops, who until then were the only ones he knew. But when he was caught driving from Holland, he was sentenced to

---

* In English in the original. A type of overland transportation of drugs, usually by car from Spain or Holland.

eight years and served seven. After his release, he went to Morocco where people tried to swindle him out of 400,000 euros in some kind of hashish scam. Hot-headed and true to his reputation, Mosquito opened fire without thinking. And that was too bad because he was sentenced to 20 years at trial, reduced on appeal to 15. Two young guys with him, also from the Plateau, got 15 too. But because they were French nationals, they were released two months later, thanks to a pardon from the king of Morocco, Mohammed VI. Mosquito, though, had never tried to become a French citizen, so he remained in prison... The other guys were the lucky ones.

Among the young guys who'd quickly moved up the ladder was Little Bombé, as I called him, from Cavée de Senlis.* He was unlucky enough to get caught with more than 500 kilos of hashish. He was 18 when I met him and lived a block away. Little Bombé was clever, intelligent, and a good car thief. He hung out with a guy nicknamed Lockjaw and they supplied us with cars. As with Mosquito, Little Bombé never sold small quantities of hashish. And just like him, he'd break into a big smile whenever I ran into him because he knew I was a thief. But he never said a thing. That was something I really liked about guys from the projects. They weren't the type to squeal. They were criminals who knew how to keep quiet.

---

* A high-rise housing project near Creil.

Bombé had started out as a mule for a wholesale dealer from the Plateau who brought in tons of shit that sold in smaller batches of 50 or 60 kilos. When he was 18, maybe 20, he got nailed in Spain where he did a stretch, about a year and a half. Once out, he decided to get into *bédo*.* He became a powerful wholesaler. After he was taken down for a half ton of hash, he escaped from a prison van in Beauvais in 2008, and he fled to Morocco. But the Moroccan special forces, which were under pressure from the French authorities, nabbed him.

When I met Mosquito *&* Bombé, I never would've thought they were the sort of guys to race off to the Netherlands, pass down through Spain, deal with dudes from the Rif in Morocco, cross the Mediterranean by speedboat, then bring all this shit to Creil. What's astonishing is that they'd never sold barrettes. They committed petty stuff, then all of a sudden they're playing big time...

But that tells you a lot about the projects. You've got delinquent kids, 16 or 17 years old, watched by the BAC.† A couple years later, they suddenly turn into *go-fasters*, crossing borders, dressing flashy and smuggling hundreds of kilos of hashish.

* Dealing joints rolled with hash, often of poor quality.
† *Brigade anti-criminalité*, part of the national police force.

What explains that?

The speed at which these kids moved, at 150 an hour. They weren't the type to sell barrettes for 15 years. It wasn't like in the 1990s, where the early *go-fasters* had been selling *bédo* for years. It didn't take these guys five years for them to understand that even a couple of kilos of cheap hash wouldn't sustain them. As soon as they got their hands on 150–200 kilos, they slashed prices. They gave absolute fuck-all about everybody else.

Older wholesalers couldn't keep up. These little gremlins ruined the biz, cutting the price by a third. With the older guys, there'd be seven or eight of them all supposed to get equal shares. Impossible with prices set by newcomers who didn't make for a gang anymore but were a regular enterprise. Two of them got richer while the rest were only underlings. The driver received a little money, another guy the same and no more. So I pay 10,000 here, 10,000 there, then walk away with 500,000 euros.

So let's go back to 1990. You weren't interested in dealing drugs but you'd had it with simple burglary. So what then?

It makes 10 years I've been stealing. So what do you know, I've got a great wardrobe, but not a dime to my name. Makes no sense.

My buddies were in the same situation. And now we've got needs. We want a driver's license, to own our own cars and have a Rolex and wear nice suits.

We went around the table. One day, three of us were meeting at McDo's at Gare du Nord. Near Barbès. I was coming from Creil and the other two had just come across Boulevard Magenta. After a bit of chit-chat, I spoke up:

—Banks! We've got to do banks!

—Fuck! You're completely crazy.

—I've found one, it's perfect, a sitting duck. I know the place inside out. There's just one woman there, all alone right in front of the vault.

—How do you figure to do it?

—What do you think? I'm going to blast it open? Am I James Caan? I'll threaten her. Just look at this!

I had a .357 Magnum on me.

—Are you fucking crazy! A Magnum!

—Listen to me. We can do it with this.

—Just one?

—It's all we need.

Where did you get that caliber pistol?

Once when robbing a bar, we'd come across it. Now we passed it around:

—Careful! It's loaded!

—Damned if you don't feel the power.

We started posing with the gun. I made like I was Jacques Mesrine. Or James Caan in Michael Mann's *Thief.**

---

* The character played by James Caan in the 1981 film is dangerous but charming.

Already Michael Mann?

One of my brothers told me about him. For us, *Thief* was our dream. A lesson in gangsterism. Among other things, you learn that thugs are nasty fuckers. We'd known as much from Jacques Mesrine's *L'Instinct de mort.** But movies were our thing. We watched *The Getaway* with Steve McQueen over and over. And *Bullitt*, even though in that film he played a cop. One of my buddies loved *Thunderbolt and Lightfoot* with Clint Eastwood. We were nuts on movies about thieves and gangsters. We were blown away by *Scarface*. When it came out we saw it 10 times. We knew all the words. That was our culture. Cinema inspired us. While committing a crime, we couldn't help repeating some line we'd heard in a movie.

What about the bank?

It was a branch of Crédit du Nord. There was no double-door security entrance, you just walked in. No cash machine, so all the money was in the till. We looked around. Should we do it? Or not? Stéphane went inside to get some change. Bruno followed & asked how he could open a bank account. We all wanted to take a look.

As it turned out, the main danger was that the teller might set off the alarm by the button under her desk. The only moment she couldn't reach it was

---

* Mesrine's 1984 memoir became the basis of the 2008 film, *Killer Instinct*.

34

when she unlocked the door to open the bank. So we absolutely had to get inside right on her heels.

—Bruno — you going?

—I'm going.

—Are you sure?

She would take five seconds to open the door. It was crucial to move fast behind her and push her inside before she could insert the videocassette in the VCR that was connected to the CCTV camera. We spent whole days watching. We bought a bag for the money. But we didn't have wigs or mustaches, nothing like that. We decided to wear caps but like idiots, didn't even know we could've bought balaclava hoods in any motorcycle store. Instead we took stockings from a sister, mother, or cousin. We were straight out of the Beagle Boys.

Finally, one morning, we were ready. But it didn't happen. The teller got there early and Bruno didn't have time to get behind her. The second time didn't work either, because she stood outside too long. The third time, Bruno got a bad feeling. Fourth time, too many people in front of the bank. The fifth, a florist across the street might've seen us. The sixth, the woman at the bakery. The seventh, a client waiting at the door. Our nerves were raw. The eighth, I just decided. I flipped out. I had to go.

—Look, I'm going inside and scare the shit out of her, then we're gone.

—Gone how? We don't have a car.

—We'll take her car!

—Fuck, McCoy. You're a genius!

My buddies didn't call me Doc yet, but McCoy. Like Doc McCoy. Steve McQueen's nickname in *The Getaway.**

Were you skipping class to rob the bank?

Yeah, I was in the last year at Jean Rostand High School in Chantilly. Not a bad student, either. I got the highest grade in French the year before the baccalaureate exam. I wouldn't actually get the bac until 2004, in prison.

Let's get back to "McCoy, you're a genius."

With the bank job happening, I started to think: the pigs are going to come after me. I'm going to get busted. I need an alibi. So I made use of school by asking the student who took care of the homework diary not to assign any for Monday morning.

We rehearsed the heist even though we had everything down by heart. At 8:50, the teller will arrive and park her car in front of the bank. Bruno keeps an eye on the florist across the street. Stéphane is my back-up & once I'm inside he waits one minute, time enough for me to open the vault. Then he'll join me. The guys all looked to me:

—What do you think?

---

* The 1971 Sam Peckinpah film, after the novel by Jim Thompson.

—Okay. But don't split and leave me inside!

—Are you nuts?

We'd bought a mallet to bust out if I got locked inside.

It so happened that the Friday before, I'd happened to walk past the bank and what did I see? A Brinks truck. Brinks — sonofabitch! Two security guys came out carrying a big bag. They loaded it inside and drove off. I thought: why rob a bank where you get just one bag of money while in a truck there's 30 or more? But that was only an outlandish dream. We were just three guys with one gun.

Monday morning, we went. The teller had barely inserted her key in the lock when I started walking. As she opened the door, I rushed over and shoved her inside. She almost lost her balance and started screaming:

—*Help me! Help!*

I'd learned my lines by heart watching the 1984 movie, *Mesrine.*

—Shut up! Do what I tell you. I've got nothing against you, I only want the money. Think of your children. Stop your bullshit or I'll kill you! Think of your children.

—*Yes, sir. Yes!*

So far, so good. We got inside.

By now I had more confidence. I realized that my big fear had completely disappeared. A little like an actor when the play begins, or a soccer star under pressure who feels at ease once on the field. You relax a bit but not too much. It's dangerous, you can easily forget where you are and what you're doing.

Once inside, I demanded she open the vault.

—Hurry up. Quick.

I spoke calmly, not yelling. She said:

—Wait, sir. The vault has an alarm.

That taught me something. Two alarms — one in the bank and another for the safe. I was becoming professional.

—Come on, open the vault. Disconnect the alarm.

She entered the code but made a mistake.

—Are you toying with me?

She finally got it open. Stéphane arrived. He didn't say a word but filled up the bag. I turned to the woman and addressed her politely:

—Miss, I've got to lock you in. And give me your car keys.

—What are you going to do with my car?

—Don't worry. You'll find it tonight in the parking lot.

Bruno, the outside lookout, joined me and Stéphane. I got in the car, drove around the block, and picked them up. Ten minutes later we were chilling in a friend's apartment.

But for me, it wasn't finished. After I parked the car and tossed the keys inside, I rushed home to change. Lacoste slacks and jacket, Weston kicks. I ran to school and found the class monitor.

—What about the diary? You didn't assign homework?

—No.

Good. I spent the day at school & in the afternoon joined my friends. They'd stayed in the apartment all day and counted the haul: 240,000 francs. Divided by three and all in cash! It was something, sure, but we didn't realize that we'd taken a giant step toward serious crime. All we knew was that we were going to hit banks! Just like when we were burglaring apartments, we weren't going to get caught. Not getting chased, no alarms, no heat from the cops, no nothing!

That same year, 1990, you had a tragedy.

Yes, my mother died of cancer. That fucked me up. I was devastated. Her death unsettled the whole family. It turned everything upside down.

I went to bury her in Algeria and when I got back, moved into my oldest sister's apartment. My father retired and returned to his village. My older brothers and sisters were married by now. I lived with my sister but Assia already had five children. She made them go without on account of me. But me, now I was loaded! With Stéphane and Bruno, I took a vacation that cost 25,000 francs. The year before my mother's death, I'd taken a summer job in a factory just to see what it was like. I hated it. But I'd realized that my mother was something else. When I left home without eating, she brought me lunch at the factory. At the end of the month, when I gave her my pay, she cried. I'd discovered something, just a little, of the world of work, and realized it wasn't the same as robbery. The money was not the same. It was unbearable. All these workers gave me the feeling that they were in for life. The factory I'd worked in was a steel mill, they carted stuff around all day, day after day. Thirty years of that and nothing else! Fuck that!

So, your mother's death made you drop out for good?

When she was in bed at the hospital, my mother gave my sister 10 francs for my bus fare. That kind of thing makes you realize what you've lost. And it's never coming back. From now on, about life, I didn't give a fuck. I didn't care for school or work. Nevertheless, I kept working. I worked in construction, building hotels at Disney World in Paris. It was hot and I worked like a fucking dog. I earned 6000 francs, but 4000 went to pay rent because now I was living alone. I didn't feel abandoned but had to wonder what comes next.

With armed robbery you found your way?

For us it was a blessing. The first job, we were armed with a pistol and we said to ourselves maybe it'll work, maybe not. But it came out fine. It brought us the same as 10 years of petty thievery combined. We borrowed lines from movies we'd seen but the self-control we'd acquired during the burglaries of apartments was what made the difference. Robbing a bank required a lot of that, & guts to boot. Because you're scared out of your wits. But it's not the kind of fear that paralyzes; it's a fear that puts pressure on you.

Like before a game. A disciplined mind, practice, and a clean healthy life were our best allies. In three minutes time we had seized 240,000 francs. Perfect gentlemen burglars, not a shot fired.

Sure, the "gentlemen burglar." But then there's the victim you've assaulted, wearing a mask and brandishing a pistol.

Let's just say: as gentlemanly as possible.

I cut you off. You were talking about your development as a criminal.

We owed our toughness to the fact that we lived with uncertainty. We questioned everything. If one of the three of us didn't like the plan we put in place, we dropped it. We had to be sure. And above all to trust one another.

After the first bank job, when I left them until evening, it never occurred to me that even a single 500-franc note would go missing. When I got back, my share was waiting.

—Dammit, Doc! We made out like Doc McCoy. Nice for you, we took the small bills and left you the big ones.

How did you spend this money?

Next day I went to Boulevard des Capucines at Opéra and bought clothes. I still remember exactly what I got: Lacoste slacks, three pair for 700 francs, and one pair of Westons for 2000 francs. I also got a belt by

Lacoste, four polo and four dress shirts. A Lacoste jacket that cost 2500 francs. Colognes, too, for which I must have paid 10,000 francs. That left me with 65,000. So I went out and bought my first Rolex, a Submariner, for 13,000 in cash. I told everybody it was a fake.

This was another world; I had plenty of money, I was flush. The neighborhood around Opéra became our headquarters. We used to meet at Café de la Paix for éclairs and hot chocolate. We got to be on first-name basis with the waiters.

Nothing in the world could make us give up on banks. They were going to fork it over. Besides, it wasn't hard. Just a week later we were already thinking about the next target.

The money went not only for chocolate éclairs, we invested in equipment: gloves, wigs, balaclavas. We bought a stopwatch and a miniature tape recorder to help with surveillance. That was risky but we destroyed the tapes soon after we listened to them. Above all, we bought a holster like Dirty Harry's.

That said, we were short on fire power. We still had just one gun. But Stéphane met with a fence he knew and told him a little white lie:

—Listen, I've got a buddy with a problem. He needs a gun.

—You call that a problem? Among thieves?

—No, not that. He's a bouncer. He wants one for self-protection.

The fence agreed to sell him weapons from his personal arsenal: a pump-action shotgun & a 9mm automatic Beretta pistol. We hid them in a storage locker we rented through an old guy we knew. We stored them in a trunk stocked with Tupperware. After that we went off to do research. That took us to FNAC, the bookstore, the section on arms and the military. We found a book about the GIGN* and studied it carefully: the weapons used, surveillance tactics, operations. It became our bible.

We also read a book about the criminal milieu in France. There was a modest history of banditry that included the big names and notorious cases. This was the stuff of inspiration.

To do what?

Banks. And their ATMs.

We watched for the arrival of the armored truck. The way it was done at the time, the truck would come, drop off money, and leave. The clerk inside the bank took the bag and refilled the ATM with cash.

A bank robbery at the time would mean being inside for half an hour to 45 minutes, so naturally we took an interest in the ATMs: how they functioned, their weak points, etc. By the time we decided to rob them, we already knew there was an electronic delay. So when we robbed an ATM the old-fashioned way, we had to stay in the bank a long time, at least

---

* GIGN (Groupe d'intervention de la Gendarmerie nationale) or the National Gendarmerie Intervention Group was the elite tactical unit of the French national police force.

45 minutes, until the time delay went off. That required a great deal of self-control. Customers would come in, the phone would ring, etc. It was important to stage a job like this with guys who were relaxed — but not too relaxed.

We decided to hit a bank near where we lived. We met in a café to watch for the truck. We didn't choose the day of the week at first but knew to avoid Wednesday because you had too many women coming in with their kids. Worse, mothers would come in for cash and leave their kids in the car, double parked on the street.

The armored trunk would arrive around 9 AM. We decided to hit the ATM between noon and 2:00 PM, when the bank was closed. We planned to grab the manager as he went home for lunch. On the day of the heist, three of us tailed his car. We wore sunglasses, gloves, false mustaches, and used walkie-talkies. We parked just next to him in the underground garage of his apartment building. When he opened his car door to get out, my partners confronted him at gunpoint. They ordered him back in the car. One of them took the wheel while the other covered him. I followed them to the bank. We went in, the four of us. By then the timer had expired, so he could open the ATM. We got 250,000 francs from the machine and inside the bank collected 200,000 on the spot. Super!

We released the manager but then, as we left, we realized that one of the employees had stayed to eat lunch at his desk. Fortunately, he hadn't realized what was going on. He thought we were just the manager's friends. We were that relaxed and confident. It reminds me of a day when I came out of a bank so well disguised that my partner didn't recognize me. It's the art of keeping cool, relaxed, and smiling. In a holdup, you've got to look calm. A guy who's tense, nervous, and sweating is not cut out for robbing banks.

My partner ordered the clerk who'd stayed for lunch into the car. We dropped him a short distance away.

From that day forward, we figured we could do both banks & their ATMs. So, we started doing these daytime robberies. The strategy was always the same. We waited for the armored trunk, then 30 minutes or an hour later we entered the bank. Why an hour? Because you might have a customer who'd give you a bad feeling. A little old lady who stayed 15 minutes, or a woman with kids. Best to wait for them to leave. Even if you stayed focused, somebody was bound to say something stupid:

—Look, while we're waiting, a couple thousand francs just disappeared.

But once started, it came off as a classic heist. One of us went in and, if need be, stood in line. If the bank had an office with smoked glass windows, two of us would go in. The first to arrive at the teller's window would give the order:

—*Hands up!*

Simultaneously one of us would barge into the office and subdue the other employees. Not first one and then the other. That's the professionalism. If either one moves too fast, it doesn't work. Almost like in an orchestra when you have to reach the high note. It happened once that we were afraid they'd triggered the alarm. These were silent alarms. We fled, not wanting to risk it. An hour later we hit another bank.

Our biggest haul from a bank heist like this was 800,000 francs. The average was around 250,000 – 300,000. Usually about every two weeks.

According to the police, you robbed some 30 banks & ATMs.

Is that what they say? What is sure and certain is that our lives changed. I had a superb apartment in Chantilly, in a residential enclave. Even bankers lived there.

Was that all you were doing?

No, we were making other scores. Computers were coming in. Was there a little something we could pull off? We'd go for it. We still had our fence. One day we learned there was a computer training center for old people who'd lost their jobs. The place wasn't guarded. So we grabbed the computers.

Not terribly glorious.

A computer went for 3000 francs. Twenty of them, 60,000. We didn't give a fuck. We were thieves!

On one of these jobs, we had something terrific happen.

We decided to go back to a place where we'd already come away with 100,000 francs. A computer store where we'd copped some Apple Mac Quadra 900s, worth about 30,000–40,000 each. Sophisticated equipment for communications companies. After the first hit, the owner installed an alarm. We disabled it and ransacked the place again. The insurance people must have gone crazy.

So then the guy installed a security camera. We'd noticed a small casement window at the back of the store. The third time, we went in at night and sawed through the bars, knowing the alarm would go off. How much stuff could we take in five minutes before the dickheads arrive? We weren't going to just drop everything and run. So we broke the window and went in full tilt: *go, go, go!* I'd become expert at disconnecting cables. We worked fast, snatched screens and CPUs, but left the keyboards. The guys from the security agency arrived just as we made it out the back. Pigs got there also, but too late.

I tried to sell the stuff to my Iranian fence, but he told me:

—You're starting to bring me too much stuff. If you want, I've got a list of brokers.

—Brokers?

—They buy used computer hardware.

At the time there was a growing black market for computers that in size rivaled the legitimate market, and eventually the BRB would become involved.*

* *Brigade de répression du banditisme* (Banditry Repression Brigade) was an arm of the national police force.

In that market, Asians had a choice piece, but they were honest and virtuous; the feujs also had a part of it. Guys from La Varenne-Saint-Hilaire, Nogent-sur-Marne, Boulogne-Billancourt — all big resellers were also looking to buy on the black market. Among them was a broker named Marc. He agreed on the spot to pay cash for all the computers I could provide. He knew they were stolen but didn't give a fuck. He rolled in a 4×4, which was not commonplace back then, and swaggered around like a thug. I didn't know it at the time but this guy, who was from Marseilles, used to rob banks himself and had done an 8-year stretch in prison.

A second fence I dealt with, in the 19th arrondissement, was also a feuj. One day I showed up at his place with some merchandise and he happened to be with a Saudi. The guy said nothing but, just when we left, he shook my hand and slipped me a Kleenex. With a phone number written on it.

Two hours later, I called him. He proposed that I deal directly with him. He was exporting to the Middle East and had already bought most of the stuff I'd sold to the fence. That's how I learned that the fence had made a huge fucking profit off me.

So when we met next, the Saudi gave me a piece of advice that would change everything...

— Why do you bother stealing the CPUs? Just take the RAM memory cards.

I've never heard of them.

—What are they?

—Computer memory. The cards aren't registered: no number, no possibility of tracing them back to you.

—And the price?

—500–600 per piece. I'll buy them for 250 each. I know where you can find 4,000 of them. They're with one of my suppliers. If you want, I'll call him and tell him I'm coming to get them. You'll have to get there before me.

That works — 4000 at 250 each… 1,000,000 francs in a single store. Can you even imagine! Just think, my friend — do the math!

The place was located in an industrial park at Porte de Saint-Ouen. A big building protected by an armored transport company, known as ACDS, a cash transportation company based in Levallois-Perret.

We cased the building. A central stairway was equipped with an intercom for entry. If you weren't an employee or regular client, you couldn't get in. So we had to find a way to slip in behind somebody. Far from easy. In a big parking lot in front of the entry there were surveillance cameras everywhere.

The company was located on the 12th floor and the entrance was equipped with an alarm. Inside you had a space with a sort of counter and room for about 10 salespeople. Across from it on the same floor, a brokerage firm was also super-secure. Between the two was an equipment room. That was the flaw — a place to hide.

To make sure we were in the right place, we went in and asked about a company that we knew was located nearby. Bruno carried a small suitcase with a video camera inside. Classic. An old trick. But we could scope out the place and become familiar with employees' faces. That was all. We left.

It all seemed too easy, according to Stéph and Bruno, and that was a problem. We went back to the Saudi and expressed our doubts. But he confirmed that there were indeed 2,500 memory cards stocked in a secure locker. He even called the guy while in front of us, who told him: "Your memory cards are here, sir. They'll be ready when you want them. Just come by."

So, we decided to do it. There were four of us & we drove out together. We went looking sharp, dressed in suits and ties, but also prepared with gloves, wigs, sunglasses, false mustaches, and micro-earpieces like what bodyguards wear, automatic pistols in holsters, briefcases packed with big sacks, nightsticks, tear gas, and Serflex metal collars to cuff everybody.

Once there, our fourth guy stayed outside as a lookout (equipped with a microphone) while I went upstairs. After reaching the control room without a problem, I called Stéphane and Bruno, then went down to let them in. We hid in the equipment room for about half an hour. It was hot. I went outside and what do I see? The two front doors to the company are wide open. Waiting for a delivery — the doors are propped open with boxes. We rushed inside. People everywhere. There must have been 30 of them.

We told everybody to lie down on the floor. Bruno used the Serflex. He was a real pro; he could cuff a person in 10 seconds. Stéph and I held everybody at gunpoint. I walked around the office and Stéph herded the employees into the center of the room. We worked quickly and closed the doors so nobody could hear. I told Stéph to stay near the entrance in case someone entered. He had a booming voice and shouted:

— *Anybody raises his head, I shoot.*

Bruno grabbed one of the employees.

— *RAM cards? Where are they?*

— What RAM cards?

First he got pistol-whipped, then I went up and rammed the barrel of the gun in his mouth.

— This is no joke. Don't play the hero. No mistake why we're here. Think of your family. Don't be stupid.

The guy brought us to the lockers. He opened them. Chock full of memory cards. I filled the 50-kilo bags. We worried they'd split open. They were a pain to carry. I called the fourth guy to come up & help. Then I stayed while the three of them carried the bags downstairs.

— Keep quiet & calm, I don't want to hear a peep. A pin drops and there'll be a massacre.

And I split.

We were now in possession of some thousands of memory cards, but now we're overcome with some serious doubt. Could the two fences, Marc and the Saudi, handle them?

Marc was the first to dispel our fears.

—RAM cards? I'll take 2000–5000 right now. Likewise with the Saudi.

—Okay. Take them and sell them.

But how could we know to trust them?

We were afraid of a trap. So it's for me to decide and I grant them my trust. These guys are all right. I gave them each a thousand pieces. They were back 24 hours later and brought us 500,000 francs. Same deal again and three hours later they're back with another 500,000. In two seconds we made like 1,000,000 francs...

We didn't have to deal with security doors & airlocks, cameras, guards, alarms connected directly to the police. They weren't afraid of theft. It was a gold mine!

We talked it over with the fences and they want more, more, more!

And it became kind of crazy. Marc gave me another address, this time in the middle of Paris.

—There you'll find at least 5,000–6,000.

I was looking at a profit of 1,200,000–1,500,000. But he added:

—They've got 2,000 pieces of 8-megabyte cards, 1,000 16-megabyte cards, 500 32 megabyte. Which are the rarest. The rest are 4-megabyte.

The 8-megabytes were going for 500 francs each, the 16 for 1,000. And so on! That was 3,000,000–4,000,000 francs. Fuck me if that's not 1,000,000 for each of us!

So we go by the address in Paris and couldn't believe it. A storefront with a little office in front and two rooms in the back where they stored the RAMs.

There was no security entrance, no airlock, not even a camera. However, there was an alarm and electric security gates. A break-in was impossible. But these guys couldn't imagine a rapid-fire heist.

After the first robbery, we bought *Le Parisien*. In the national edition, nothing. But in the local edition we read that the anti-gang unit was in charge of the investigation. The cops were going to be on the trail of computer criminals but they're going to need a couple of years. Meanwhile, we can make a real killing.

For the Banditry Repression Brigade (BRB), you're big-time...

The BRB had no clue. Hold-ups grabbing millions, the computer market. Was it stealing computers? Like us, they'd never heard of RAM cards. But they figured out fast that it was the kind of robbery to meet demand. They would need to infiltrate the black market. They'd tap broker's phones, catch a few of the small-time fences. But it wasn't a world they knew, not part of the traditional criminal milieu. Yet it was indeed armed robbery and they had no doubt they were dealing with professional thieves.

We were ready for a second hit. On the appointed day, I was the first customer at 9 AM. I open the door and go in. There's a guy on the phone. I grab the receiver from him and hang it up. My partners follow while one of them, in dark glasses and disguised with a fake mustache and wig, goes to distract the old lady who runs the store across the street and is always watching.

We go to the back; everything is in boxes. But they're too big so we have to open and unpack them. That takes an hour and a half. The *sang-froid* you acquire from bank heists is helpful. When the phone rings, we don't answer. When a customer arrives, boom, we grab and take him to the back room and hold him there with the others. Then we leave. We sell everything in a couple of weeks and come away with 1,250,000 francs each. We're like oil barons. We go see the fences.

—You want more?

—More and more... We're sending them out of the country. To Morocco, Jordan...

Two weeks later, another job. The gold rolls in.

But what did you do with all the money? Why risk prison when you had so much?

We bought big jars of jam and preserves. We emptied them and put the money inside. We didn't want to leave it in bags: we were afraid it would be gnawed by rats. We dug a hole and buried it. That's how we kept the money.

What did we do with it? Rolexes for us and our girlfriends. Fancy clothes. Black and brown Westons, golf shoes, fancy leather belts... We rented apartments. My two partners opted for upscale Paris neighborhoods.

How could you do that without pay stubs?

It wasn't hard. A friend of mine was doing really well. He opened a bank account for me in his name and used checks to pay rent, gas and electricity. He visited the real estate agencies in Chantilly and explained to one of them that he required total confidentiality because he was thinking of renting a kind of love nest. He paid six months in advance plus the security deposit and got the keys right away so he could go there with his girlfriend. It was a high-end building with a terrace and underground parking.

Using the same cover, I bought a BMW 325i convertible. I gave my friend cash and he paid from his bank account. Of course, I pay him with gifts of clothes, jewelry, colognes — added to which, he took his 15%. He had no problem with earning an easy 60,000 francs.

As for my partners, they bought a Porsche and a Lamborghini Diablo. Same deal as me: they found a well-to-do friend to whom they paid cash.

Sure, but wasn't that sort of conspicuous...

Yeah, as we quickly realized, and in everyday life we began keeping a low profile. For cars, in fact, we turned to little Renault Clios or the Peugeot 306. We'd still change a few times a year, but nobody noticed. We always dressed in suits and ties and passed for salesmen.

We also spent a lot of money feeding our families, filling up fridges for brothers and sisters. But also lots of useless stuff. We spent days shopping, buying a ton of records and going to the movies. Money went out the window fast; we didn't know what it was anymore. We didn't even look at price tags.

Since we didn't have vices — alcohol, drugs, or prostitutes — we traveled. First thing, I invited my partners to Algeria. They hesitated: "Those Arabs, they're going to cut our throats." But then they accepted, to my great surprise. Stéphane took the opportunity to make a pilgrimage to his grandfather's grave, which was in Algiers. When they went back to Paris, they in turn suggested that I go with them to visit their families in Israel.

—Are you game?

I accepted on the spot. And after that trip, we went to New York. There we stayed in grand style: the Waldorf Astoria and the Four Seasons, a helicopter tour of Manhattan. We celebrated a girlfriend's birthday inside the crown of the Statue of Liberty, where we had a birthday cake delivered. We visited Las Vegas and booked the same suite we saw in *Rain Man* with Dustin Hoffman and Tom Cruise, at $3500 a night. We went from Las Vegas to Los Angeles by convertible. After that we flew to South Africa, Israel, and back to Europe: Spain, Switzerland, England, Belgium, and the Netherlands... Stéphane and Bruno hit all the islands with their girls: Tahiti, the Maldives, Seychelles, Reunion, the West Indies, Hawaii... They also went to China and Australia.

We had so much bread sometimes we even forgot where we'd stashed it. It's crazy. One time, in my bathroom, I came across a bottle of XS Paco Rabanne. It was packed with Swiss francs: 30 gold bars I'd completely forgotten.

I handed out wads of cash right and left. One day I was supposed to meet Marc at Café de la Paix, where he was going to give me 800,000 francs. We always worked the same way: I'd leave the merchandise in the trunk of my car in the parking lot at Opéra, he'd take the stuff & pass me the cash. That day I was with two buddies from Creil, Naïm & Karim, who by the way, when under interrogation, would prattle on about my lifestyle. Just because I didn't want them seeing the 800,000 francs, I gave them a fistful of cash so they'd go off to buy clothes for themselves and their girlfriends.

You could have become simply well-off, owning a restaurant or a bar.

Stéphane and Bruno invested in land in Israel, in a restaurant and real estate. They were clever. Not me. I still just kept hiding money. You get so used to living the life of a thief, become so taken with the smell of gold, that you want to keep doing it and never stop. It's pathological; you're sick but don't know it. Later, in prison, you think about it and take a step back. And find some answers. When I went to spend a month or two in Israel, my friends and I got bored. There was no action. One day, instead of going jet skiing or scuba diving, we got a notebook to plan out our next hits.

The problem, in fact, was our lack of vices. Without realizing it, we'd become dependent on the adrenaline rush you get from robbing banks. We were addicts. On vacation, we'd have anxiety attacks, like we were jonesing.

We also were seriously passionate about work that was well done. Always looking to make ever more sophisticated heists. We carefully broke down plans and examined them, tried to plan ahead for everything. Success meant nobody got killed or wounded, so everybody could go home — we'd have the feeling of making robbery almost scientific.

Did your methods often change?

Once, when we were getting ready to pull off a job, Stéphane took me aside:

—Doc, why should we take risks when we go inside? Why not just take hostages?

—You're right: we'll grab the boss...

We went off to the Chamber of Commerce to get the company's K-bis.* They didn't even ask for identification, and often let you have it for free. With this document, you knew the name and address of the company manager.

---

* In France, a registered document that certifies a company's compliant status.

So now we go to the place and spot a Mercedes. That's got to be his. He's the one who closes up at night and opens in the morning. Okay, so next morning we go to his house.

Same game:

—Think about your family, don't play the hero. We're not giving out party favors. You've got insurance. We're only interested in your goods. What do you have? Where is it? What's the layout of the place? What's the code to turn off the security cameras?

We go with him and he deactivates the code. We dive in, bingo! 5,000 RAM cards. From our fences we get cash. Works like a charm.

For another hit, near Levallois-Perret, we brought in a new recruit, Jérémie. The guy was a regular atomic bomb. He came from the Creil Plateau. He was smart, courageous, and clever, with great *sang-froid*. We'd scoped him out and already tapped him for one hit. For this one, he also provided the cars. He got them with the help of neighborhood buddies who were specialists.

Once at the scene, while we were still waiting in the car, we saw the company manager come out and walk over to a building across the street. Leaving his office empty.

—Let's go!

We hid inside the bathroom and waited. Five minutes later, he's back with five women and they go to work in the office. We've taken off our shoes and go barefoot up the stairs. We rob the place. They have some RAM, not a lot. But in the vault we find something else: *microprocessors*.

We didn't know what they were but the fact that they were in a vault meant they were worth a lot of money. We took everything. In fact, we didn't know it, but a Pentium microprocessor at the time cost 6,000 francs. That very morning we'd copped around 9,000 of them.

We went to see Marc & the Saudi. We sold them at 1,000 per piece. Do the math... It's like a billion.

After that, we told ourselves we had to do another super-fucking job! We took vacations, spent a lot, and stashed the rest. This was 1995 and I was 23 years old. Come December and I'm saying, "It's been a long time since I robbed a bank." The others thought I was nuts.

—You can't be serious!

—On my mother's grave, it's been too long since we hit a bank. You want to come? You don't? No problem, I know other guys from the neighborhood who will.

I went with Jérémie and another guy from Creil. We targeted the local BNP. This other guy would later squeal on me...

That was my problem: I was bursting with adrenaline; I couldn't sit still. The other guys went on vacation but, me, everything that wasn't nailed down, I wanted to steal.

Did you mingle with punks like yourself from the *cité*?

Yeah, sometimes I worked without the "Parisians," also known as the "Feuj Connection" of Barbés. That was the case with the BNP in Creil, located in Cavée de Senlis.* I never met a bank robber who hadn't gone after his own local branch or that of his parents. That was a famous rule never to be broken. With all the money from stealing RAM, my Paname pals couldn't understand why I needed to keep hitting banks. They were convinced that I was just looking for trouble; maybe they were right. But at the time I was young and unusually successful at this kind of thing.

Did you imagine you were invincible?

I thought I could handle any situation. Yeah, you feel, or rather, you believe you're invulnerable and are quite certain that nothing can happen to you. It's not true, of course, but it was just that feeling of power that enabled you to move up the ranks.

You couldn't let it go. So another bank... Tell us about it.

When you rob your own bank, it's really very simple: you know the place by heart! No need to learn who the employees are, or even their first names, or the office layouts or hours. Nothing to prepare. When D-day comes, of course, you can't let on just how well you know the place.

* See p. 30.

Why?

Cops are far from stupid... They'll spot any kind of collusion right away and suspect the thief has an account in the bank. They know the standard stuff. When you do a stick-up, you consider two things: the best way to do your job and the police investigation to come. If you figure out how to solve both, you're not going to pay the price.

For the BNP, it was December. Thieves are always fond of Christmas. We found out where the boss lived. With two buddies from Creil, we all went wearing masks. One of us went as Santa Claus. It was a Tuesday evening.

Santa rang the bell. The boss opens the door to find himself facing Father Christmas and the barrel of a gun. Meanwhile, the rest of us gather around: François Mitterrand, Jacques Chirac, Valéry Giscard D'Estaing. Now we're all in the living room. And there it's like in the movies: *"Good evening! Good evening! We're your former presidents!"* We put up our hands, make the "V for victory" gesture. Gifts for the whole family. Chocolate and candy galore. Laughter and good cheer. The holidays are here. Anything goes!

So you made as if you were in a movie?

Except that it wasn't. The boss realized it fast. But, to answer your question, I was inspired by the film *Point Break* with Keanu Reeves. It's the story of thieves who wear masks, disguised as former American presidents, when they go after California banks. In fact, when I left the boss's place to go to the bank, I waved good-bye and borrowed a line from the movie: *"Thanks! Your vote means a lot to me!"*

What happened then?

After spending the night in the banker's house, I left at 7:30 in the morning to pick up a Renault Express with tinted windows that I'd parked in front of the security entrance to the bank. The van with my partner hiding in the back, equipped with a walkie-talkie. For 10 minutes I waited, out of sight in the entrance to the adjoining building, just in case somebody who might be watching from the window saw what we were up to. Then I returned to the boss's place. There I quickly explained:

—I'm not going to hurt you or your family. But if you do anything stupid, you and everybody else are going to be in deep, deep shit. You especially. Everything is going to go just fine. Or else very, very badly. It's your choice. Don't try to play the hero. We're going to the bank and you'll do just as I say. Okay?

—No problem, Mister!

We took his car and I told him to be sure not to look at me. I was dressed like him: suit and tie, briefcase, polished shoes. But different, too, what with my hairpiece, fake mustache, and glasses. Before we left the house, I told my partner who was staying with the family that I'd be calling him on the cell phone as soon as we were done.

I park in front of the bank. I'm listening to my walkie-talkie, which I keep out of sight below my belt. I call the guy in the lookout van:

—Can you hear me?

—Just fine! Don't leave the car just yet. There's the cleaning woman at the butcher's. She's taking out the trash.

I order the boss to drive around the block. But he's got to be quiet about it. We stay calm. We see that the cleaning woman has left the front door to the butcher shop open. She could come out again at any moment. I made him park the car but not look in the direction of the butcher shop. The woman might start a conversation and I don't see myself inviting her for coffee. He parks and we get out.

—Smile while you're walking. You're happy and off to the job. Act like nothing's wrong.

He played the game and gave me a smile.

—Super. Keep it up. All the way to the entrance. But don't look at me.

Just in front of the door was the bus stop for Cavée de Senlis. And who should be standing there at 8 A M but a guy I knew. My friend Karim. Nice guy from "Chicago," as his Creil neighborhood was known. I liked him a lot; we used to do petty larceny stuff when I was younger. Was he going to recognize me? He glanced our way but didn't react. A relief, because he was just the kind of crazy-ass who, if he knew what you were up to, would want to join us. Close call.

We entered the bank at 8:15 AM. If we'd gone in earlier, we would've triggered a silent alarm. The boss disconnected the alarm system. I told him to immediately call security at the main BNP branch and use his normal voice... He complied and dialed the number, gave the password, and hung up. So far, everything's gone as planned. About 8:30, my earpiece buzzes:

—The blonde is arriving...

I send the boss to open the door. His colleague enters and I very calmly explain the situation. She takes a seat usually reserved for customers. Roles reversed — this morning I'm the boss. I keep reassuring them. At no time do I aim my .357 at them. It stays in the holster — the same type as Belmondo has in *Peur sur la ville!** — and now it's 8:50:

—Can you hear me? The other woman's coming...

Same game. The boss opens the door for the second employee. Again I explain what's going on. But this lady freaks out more than the first one. I bring her inside. She's in panic mode. The boss helps me calm her down. Normally, he would have picked her up in the morning. Fortunately, I'd thought to bring a phone with a speaker so that when I told him to call her last night, he'd asked her to take a cab to work because his car was in the shop. Now she knew the real reason.

* *Fear Over the City,* a 1975 crime film directed by Henri Verneuil and starring Jean-Paul Belmondo.

This all takes a while. Now what do you do? Take the money and leave?

Not just yet, pal! The branch opens its doors at 9:00 and only at 9:10 can the vault alarms be turned off.

What did you do about the customers?

I gave the boss a marker and told him to write on a piece of paper: "THIS BRANCH WILL OPEN THIS MORNING AT 10:00 A M." No sooner said than done. He did exactly what I asked and taped the paper to the glass door. I had him do it — above all, not me. DNA testing was just starting and it scared the living shit out of me. Two or three customers came to the door and left after reading the note. It worked.

The manager turned off the vault alarm and called security at the main branch. Everything was going as planned. We opened the vaults. No less than 200,000 francs. We turned off the ATM alarm and from the machine took a little more than 300,000. Then we cut the video surveillance alarm. The hitch was, though, this one had a timer. We had to wait 30 minutes more. Customers kept coming to the bank, reading the note and leaving. My accomplice in the van kept me apprised of their comings and goings. It's 9:45. Now the manager was getting scared. Once the surveillance timer shut off, he wasn't able to make the videocassette eject. He panicked, thinking I'd get upset. I calmed him down, explaining that the machine was now turned off. So I quietly asked him to go to the entrance and open the first security door. Stepping on the door mat would trigger the video recorder. He was flabbergasted I'd know that and wondered how. Maybe, *my friend,* because I've watched too many gangster movies. I now thanked everybody for their collaboration and brought out the Smith and Wesson handcuffs, the kind you can only find in the United States. The cops would be amused by that. I didn't double lock them tight, and while leaving I saw an employee freeing her hand to take a cigarette. I stared. She slipped her hand back in the cuff. I gave her a smile, then called my partner:

— Coast clear? Can I come out?

— Let's go, pal. *Vamos!*

Outside, I took the boss's car. The van followed. He'd pick up our partner at the boss's apartment building. I call him on a portable phone bought just for this job.

— Hey, it's me. Everything's good. Be there in two minutes. *Tchao.*

While we were doing the bank, he'd been packing everything into a garbage bag, including the speakerphone, Santa Claus costume, the masks…

To confuse the police, I abandoned the boss's car in the direction of Paris and walked back through a neighborhood in Creil. I made it to the hideout where the others would join me.

— Robbing a bank these days! What a mess you've got to make!

It's not like in the '80s.

Here's where I understand my Paname buddies. It's true; they're right. We've got to stop hitting banks. But what can I say? I wasn't exactly Snow White. And I was pretty foolish.

At least you had the satisfaction of a job well done?

Not even. It's not a normal job that would let you feel that way. To be sure, the fact that nobody gets hurt was a real relief. But we naively thought we weren't doing any harm. We thought of thievery as trickery. A con job, nothing serious.

Even though it's violent and extremely dangerous.

There's the threat of violence, certainly; I agree. But for me, at the time, it was nothing but bluff. It was all based on psychology. We applied pressure at the start of a job, then relaxed. You've just got to stay calm, which reassures the client as to our intentions. He knows his best chance is to do as we ask. That's why he doesn't try anything stupid. It was all a big con job in the end, because the threat wasn't real. At the slightest fuckup, we would've taken off in a hurry without a second thought.

In the heat of the moment, victims don't know that.

No, and at the time I didn't weigh the extent of the psychological damage I caused these people. Even when you don't hurt anybody during these jobs, it's obvious that you traumatize them. I only realized that when I found myself facing them in criminal court. The simple fact of pointing a gun at somebody — even a fake one — can cause permanent damage.

Do you regret it?

I was really young. Can you turn back the clock and re-live the past? Time machines don't exist. I'm not going to play the redeemed soul for you by express-ing endless regret.

Let's get back to business. After the BNP holdup in Creil, you decided to not get mixed up with things there again, but do jobs only with your Parisian partners?

No, not yet! A rich fence who specialized in jewelry happened to turn up, and he had plenty of cash. He'd pay for stolen merchandise at 10% its value, two-thirds in cash on delivery, the rest two months later. That's the way it always works. Which made me want to go after a jewelry store, even though it's a very risky job. The merchandise is so hot. You've got to meet with the fence several times, always with the risk that this so-called merchant might be tracked by the cops. When a jewelry store gets robbed, the pigs put intense pressure on all the fences they know. It's the only way to nab the thieves. And most of all, they're trying to recover the jewels. Insurance com-panies push hard for a full investigation. The police had spun a web around France and across Europe. They knew the players in Paris, but also Anvers. With this kind of loot, you've got to be super careful.

Did the Paname guys join you on this one?

Absolutely not. They told me I was completely nuts. They called me "radioactive" and stayed away from me. I was hopeless. They didn't try to argue with me anymore. They gave up. At all events, they were off to the South Pacific for two months, on a beach beneath the palm trees, doing nothing. Stéphane liked to talk about his vacations. Fishing, seashells, sunsets...

Far as I was concerned, you could keep your fish and chips. Have a nice vacation! But it won't be with me. I've got a movie to shoot in Chantilly!

This was the giant jewelry store there?

That's right. It's the most beautiful store in the entire region. The bourgeois from the racetrack at Chantilly and Lys de Lamorlaye all flock there — wealthy owners, jockeys, and also the likes of Agha Kan. *Créme de la créme* millionaires. I knew the city because I'd been a student at the high school there. Also, I'd often help out the father of a friend from Creil. Some Moroccan Jews ran a clothing stand in the market, which was not far from the jewelry store. His old man needed help packing up the merchandise, and sometimes my friend couldn't go because he had to study.

At the time I'd never noticed the jewelry store. It was a beautiful surprise to find it located in a neighborhood I knew well!

How did you decide on this place?

The store is located in the middle of downtown. Unless you do a quiet break-and-enter à la the *Pink Panther*, I don't see how you can avoid the "raid" approach. We'll target the store's manager and get him at his house. Problem was the guys from Creil who were joining me on this expedition, they weren't cut from the same cloth as Stéphane and Bruno, who were purebred attack dogs — alert, fast, and amazing self-control. The guys from Creil were not as professional and had less courage. Followers more than leaders. So I decided we'd go about things quietly but run the same movie as with BNP. For me, this was now the standard approach. The hardest part was to learn where the boss lived and get him inside without attracting attention. It took several days of observation and tactical tailing to know who was in charge, whether he in fact had the keys to the place, and where he lived.

Can you explain what you call tactical tailing?

When you observe the routine around opening and closing a store, you quickly learn employees' various levels of responsibility. One always stands out from the others. Always. When it comes to security, that's the great weakness. They have no choice but to confer trust upon certain human beings. A lesson I learned from an older guy in Creil, a master thief. His motto was, "Anything that can be locked shut can be opened, it only takes finding the flaw." Technology or no, there's always a human being involved. That's the weak link.

Then, in order to know where the person in question lives, you've got to tail him. For that, you use several vehicles and are ready to work at night when the store closes. Even if you have three cars equipped with walkies-talkies, you don't want to risk following your target home. Jewelers are extremely suspicious. So we used three cars, took turns, and tracked him each for half a mile, then stopped. The next day we started from that point, and continued that way until we made it to the place where he lived. Once we had the address, the plan was to park a van in front of his house and another not far from the store.

How did you learn to do all this?

In 1993, when the Carabinieri nabbed Toto Riina,* the Big Boss of the Cosa Nostra in Sicily, they described for the newspapers how they'd set up the tactical tail that led to his capture. Slow and steady, step by step... *"Piano-piano"* as they say in Italy. And we read the papers.

---

* The Italian national police force. Riina, the "boss of bosses" in the Italian mafia, had been a fugitive since the 1960s. His capture was a sensational national news story.

To really master the technique, we spent hours training on the Paris *périphérique*. We chose targets randomly and tailed them with three cars. Until we got as good as the boys in blue!

And with all this effort, what exactly did you hope to get?

Knowing the guy had keys to both the store in Chantilly and the other one in downtown Creil, we were going to come away with no less than 50,000,000 francs, or nearly 8,000,000 euros. That's a lot of beautiful jewelry. We planned to do it à la *Reservoir Dogs*. Just like in Quentin Tarantino's film. When talking in front of the employees, we'd be addressing one another by color: *Mr. Yellow, Mr. Green, Mr. White...*

The rest was simple. We decided to grab the manager in the basement of his building.

After leaving the store, he arrives at the entrance to the underground parking garage at about 7:15 PM. We enter on his tail and wait until he parks his car. The place is deserted and we corner him. I'm at the wheel of our car and demand the garage door remote. Then we leave like we came and I drive across town while two others stay in the van with the manager. But he plays the tough guy and refuses to cooperate. You get the feeling he's going to play the hero.

Going upstairs with this fool is not a risk worth taking. So with my friend from high school, alias Mr. White, we go up to the apartment. I have the keys & as I go to unlock the door, I hear his wife: *"Is it you?"*

I'm startled and reply, *"Yeah, it's me."* As soon as she opens the door, I cover her mouth to keep her from screaming. I drag her into the living room and tell her I'm going to take my hand away, but she shouldn't even think of screaming. Nodding her head, she agrees. I give her the usual:

—We're not here to hurt you, Miss. I'm not going to do anything to you. The jewelry store is the only thing that interests me. If I'm holding keys to your apartment, that's because we've got your husband downstairs. We know everything about you and everything about the stores. Tomorrow morning all this will be over. So don't do anything stupid. Okay?

Almost bizarrely, she seems reassured. She's not exactly relaxed, but she stays calm. She can take the stress. I note this immediately & so don't tie her up. No need for handcuffs.

But is it really as simple as that? It's enough that you talk and people listen?

Once again, it's a question of method. I think of it as a duel during which I use the threat of force to intimidate. You've got to convince the other person that you're stronger and it would be a mistake to resist. The real subtlety in this approach was to bring her to the point of making the choice herself. She "chooses" to take your side for survival's sake. If done right, people will do everything possible to help you succeed — their life depends on it. Often they even tell you things you didn't know. You've not only solved a problem but strengthened your team with an excellent new recruit.

From what movie did you get this Machiavellian notion?

None. It's professionalism. You can't last long in armed robbery if you're a pea-brained idiot. You've got to master all aspects: how to case a job, how to analyze the situation, the protagonists, the power dynamics, and finally the execution — which will improve with experience. For all this you've got to be open-minded, learn from others, listen, read, and stay informed. But to answer your question, no, it didn't come from a movie this time. It happened that I got into a discussion between my brother and one of his friends. They were enthusiastic students of geopolitics and military strategy. For example, during the Gulf War they spent nights analyzing Operation Desert Storm with all sorts of references to strategy. One of them stuck in my memory: *Strategy involves using all possible means to bring about the enemy's moral and psychological disintegration in order to convince him that continuing to fight is useless.* Shatter the will to resist. It's exactly the same method that competent police use to break a suspect in custody, to get his cooperation and obtain a confession. Not like others who suppose that torment and abuse will make a suspect confess. Physical violence doesn't work with everybody. In my robberies there was a phase of "custody" with "interrogation." I didn't invent any of this. I just used best practices and adapted them to my work. That's all.

Okay, so you're inside the jeweler's apartment and his wife is calm. What happens now?

She's sitting on her couch. I turn on the television. I give her a glass of water. She stays calm, quietly watching TV. I tell Mr. White to stay with her while I let the others know that everything's gone well so far. I take the car and drive toward the soccer stadium, which is where I'm going to meet with the second team. I drive past the jewelry store downtown:

— *Got you, bitch! Tomorrow we party!* I'm all alone and screaming: *Aïe, aïe, aïe!*

From my pocket I take out the key rings. They contain all the keys to the doors and vaults of both jewelry stores. I squeeze them tight. I'm holding the *Open Sesame!* to Ali Baba's cave in my hand. You can't imagine how happy it makes me. More than jewels, my mind rocks with thought of the gems and gold bars that must be in the vault. I trip out, day-dreaming like crazy. I think of Stéphane and Bruno. Too bad they're not here! I'll make sure they get something out of this anyhow, no matter what.

So what next? I'm guessing it's to go down like at BNP. You're to leave with the manager early next morning and empty the vaults.

Exactly. But I get to the stadium toward 9:00 that night with two others only to find D***, alias Mr. Yellow, is roughing up the manager. Who he's got hand-cuffed. I tell him to stop.

—What this about?

—He's playing the smart aleck.

—So? You want to fucking kill him?

I'm pissed off. There's nothing worse than a hostage who's petrified with fear. That can make him do anything. At all events I never used physical violence.

—The man's in cuffs, no need for anything else.

To the manager I say:

—Don't try to be clever & you won't get hurt. I've been to your place and everything's gone well there.

I show him an object I've taken from inside his apartment.

—You play stupid and I'll play stupid, too. So it's in your best interest to do what we ask. Ok?

The guy acquiesces. I reassure him, repeating that nobody wants to hurt him. But now I've got to leave. The two others will stay with him until morning, when I'll come by at 9 A M. I go back to his place. Everything is going as planned. From downstairs I call Mr. White. He tells me he's downstairs, too. In fact, I can see him a good ways off. I park the car.

—What the fuck is going on?

This idiot tried to impress the woman by loading his revolver. A shot went off — but so why did he leave? We had the television turned on. But this shitass turned if off. He doesn't have time to explain because now here come the cops. We can't go back to the car at this point, they're right in front of the building. Mr. White wants to run off toward the city center — two birds like us, dressed in black suits with black boots and automatic pistols.

So I take control of the situation. We'll try hiding somewhere around the building. Chantilly police are anything but sissies: they've got roadblocks, spike strips, motorcycles, assault rifles... If we run into them, we're toast. Except that, after a while, nothing. Not a single cop, nowhere to be seen. I seize the opportunity to run back to the car and jump behind the wheel and back up. But a little police van comes right in front of us, then I notice a patrol car with its lights off. In a fraction of a second I shift out of reverse to escape as it tries to block our way. But I was fast. If the car had stalled when shifting gears, we'd be dead in the water. A real ambush.

The cops jump out of their van, guns drawn. They're to my left and my window is down. I raise my hands and Mr. White does the same. The car's still inching forward and suddenly I shift into gear and step on it. A burst of gunfire. The back windshield explodes and we hear blasts from the automatic Berettas. We duck down and I drive blind. It's straight out of Colt Seavers!* After 500 feet the tires go flat. We jump out and sprint onto some nearby railroad tracks.

It's night. The cops are brave but not foolhardy. They're not going to chase two armed suspects in pitch darkness...

---

* The 1980s American action-adventure television series, *The Fall Guy*, features actor Lee Majors as Colt Seaver, a movie stunt man and bounty hunter.

Soon I find myself in the courtyard of my high school — I know the place. To get to the stadium to pick up the others, I've got to keep out of sight. The only way is to cross the Château de Chantilly. Walking, it's at least five kilometers, not to mention security, canine patrols, and roadblocks. Then there's Mr. White. The stupid fucker doesn't want to go that way and decides to go directly back home. Abandoning our partners. We start to argue in the middle of the Chantilly forest but he pretends not to hear me and runs off through the woods.

Just as an aside, later on, it wouldn't take the jerk half a minute before talking about me when the gendarmes had him in custody. The guy was white in name only.

How did you react in the moment? Because I find it under-standable that your accomplice, given the gendarme's *Plan Épervier*,* might not want to die. Cops were shooting at you. He had to be feeling the heat.

I swear that, at the time, I didn't realize it. Only one thing freaked me out: the two guys and the jeweler in the van not knowing that things had gone south and the cops were ready to shoot on sight. At the chateau, I got inside the courtyard. Okay so far. The security guys are not busy tonight. They're asleep at the

---

* A high alert issued by French national police in such cases as kidnapping and prison escape, which amounts to an order to "shoot to kill."

wheel. Fortunately for them, I'm not here to steal the tapestries or great masterworks... And whose tracks do I cross in the park but Mr. White! The asshole has got himself cornered beside the lake. He can't climb the fence because 10 yards away there's a roadblock with 20 cops.

I undress. Bare feet and underwear. He does the same. We cross the freezing fucking lake with our clothes above our heads. We did it just like it happens to Gian Maria Volonté in *Le Cercle rouge*. Which shows you that cinema doesn't just influence but it also inspires. If my professor was Michael Mann, Jean-Pierre Melville was my technical adviser...*

When we reach the other side, we're like frozen fish sticks. I use my undershirt to dry myself. Then we dash through the woods along the highway leading to the stadium. I'm sick to my stomach that I won't find the others alive & that trigger-happy cops may have even killed the jeweler. I come near the stadium, concealed behind bushes. I glance right & left, then charge straight into the van. The three of them are there. They know nothing about what's happened.

We leave the jeweler inside the van and head back into the woods. I'm so happy to see Belkacem (alias Mr. Green) that I blink back tears. I like the guy and would feel guilty if anything happened to him. On the way back, on foot through the woods to Creil,

---

* *Le Cercle rouge,* a 1970 film directed by Jean-Pierre Melville that involves a jewelry store heist.

I told him about idiot number one, who'd provoked the whole disaster, and also idiot number two, who'd punched out the jeweler for no reason. Both guys would one day rat us out for this botched job.

Lesson of the day: fucked-up human resources! And a problem that would never end because in this kind of work, good thieves are hard to find...

Reaching Creil, walking along the banks of the Oise, I took the keyrings from my pocket. With a heavy heart, I tossed them into the river. Treasure's gone and I want to cry.

Did you tell your usual accomplices about this disaster?

They made fun of me. For a year all I heard was: "Great team you've got, Doc!" & "You're a true mastermind!" & "Next time, invite us. Always happy to work with real professionals." They kept teasing me like that but, at the same time, when they learned the whole story, about the shooting & the rest, they got very worried and stopped being so smug.

And did you get back together with them?

After the bank heist, Stéphane, Bruno, and I planned a job that would be a gold mine. A factory called Kingline in Aulnay-sous-Bois was the source for major suppliers of memory cards. Same game: get the K-Bis from the Bobigny Chamber of Commerce near the courthouse. The manager lived in Créteil and the factory was located in the freight zone at

Roissy-Charles de Gaulle Airport. My brother Fayçal, who had seen how I was making a ton of money, was busting my balls. He wanted in. He pestered me so much that I finally agreed. I also recruited another guy from Creil. Our friend Jérémie also joined us. That made six.

I scoped the apartment where the female manager lived, and figured we'd hide in a nearby stairwell. As soon as she opened the door, we'd go in commando-style. We'd be in jumpsuits and balaclavas but also bulletproof vests, because cops at the time were quick to shoot. We also bought walkie-talkies with ear receivers, automatic pistols with holsters, etc. We planned to get into the building with the postman's master key. Stéphane, wearing a wig and dressed in suit and tie, would wait in front of the building to let us know when the woman arrived.

How did you manage to get firearms?

Through guys in the projects. We had some guns, mostly pistols and revolvers from break-ins. Kids from the *cité* would come to see us:

—Take a look at this .357 Magnum. I stole it from a cop's apartment.

—How do you know he'a a cop?

—Well, who else keeps a .357 at home?

—Get out of here! He might be a collector. What makes you think a cop keeps a 44 Magnum at home?

Those we did get, we never bothered to test. We didn't care, they were just for show and to scare people. If the cops turn up, they're going to shoot and we'll have to take somebody hostage. Otherwise we're fucked. Hostages were our thing, we'd use them as shields.

That's risky.

You've got no choice. It's your only way out.

You could surrender.

Completely out of the question!

Okay, let's go back to what happened.

Three of us are in the stairwell on the top floor of the building. Outside are Jérémie, Stéphane, and Bruno. The car arrives. They let us know. We go down to the second floor. The elevator door opens. It's an Asian couple. They turn the key in the door. As soon as it opens I shout:
    —Go!
We shove them inside thinking they're only two. But what the fuck: we run into the grandfather and grandmother — and eight of them altogether. A total mess! Bad information! We're in deep shit.

We told them to stay calm. We didn't cuff them. No blows, insults, or slaps — nothing unnecessary. We try to keep things running smoothly. If we make our intentions clear from the start, it will work out. It's the woman who's important. I take her separately into a bedroom:

—Here's the situation, Miss. We're going to Aulnay to empty the vaults. We're just here for the memory cards.

—You want to steal computers?

—We don't care about the computers. Just the RAM.

—I see. But what about the supervisor of the room where the vaults are kept?

In fact, there was a huge roomful of vaults, protected by an armored door, a pair of surveillance alarms, & the company's own video cameras. There was also the Roissy airport freight zone security system: a double-door security entrance, sections off-limits to employees, a green zone... The works.

I explained to the woman that we'd be going tomorrow morning, and see for ourselves.

The next day, over my bulletproof vest, I put on the suit I'd brought in a garment bag, and gave the woman instructions:

—Miss, you're not to look at me, ever. Not ever. Not even once.

We left my brother and one of the guys with the family. We'd call them after cleaning out the vaults. I drive the woman's car and arrive in Aulnay, where we park next to a little Renault Express that we'll use to transport the merchandise. We silence the alarms and Jérémie goes upstairs to keep an eye on whoever comes & goes.

We can't open the door that leads into the main room, to be sure, but there are toilets in the back. I go inside and remove the tiles from the drop ceiling. I slip inside, then do the same with tiles in the vault room. I drop down inside and open the door. We fill the bags with memory cards but at this point the phone rings. A problem in the apartment in Créteil.

What's happening? The family's 20-year-old son tried calling the family all night. Not getting an answer, in the morning he came by to see what was going on. He had a key and so took my partner and my brother by surprise. They drew their guns but the guy wasn't alone. His girlfriend was behind him in the doorway and they didn't see her at first. She managed to get downstairs just when a police car happened to pass by. My partner managed to escape but my brother, after he stashed the bags with the balaclava and overalls behind some bushes, was captured near the apartment building...

We rushed from the factory, leaving most of the merchandise. But with plenty of time to think about what went wrong in our planning...

With your brother's arrest, the anti-crime unit that was investigating some 11 hostage-related hold-ups of computer firms now had a substantial lead.

Fayçal was taken into custody by the regional judicial police force (the SDPJ of Val-de-Marne)* before his case was consigned to the anti-crime unit in Paris. Fayçal was a kid from the projects who'd never been in custody, much less in prison. We wondered if he'd talk. But he showed that boys from the *cité* can be solid. He didn't give his first or last name. He stayed

---

* The criminal investigation arm of the national police force.

mute like that for some 10 hours. But the cops he had to deal with were not representative of the BRB. Later I'd meet many of them and they were much more decent. These guys smashed in my brother's face. They broke some of his teeth and his face was a mess. According to the report, he'd been hysterical and banged his head against the wall.

—*Dirty Arab raghead scum! Tell us your name.*

He kept his mouth shut the time he knew it would take us to get back home and clean things up. They didn't break him later on, either. He simply told them:

—My name is Fayçal Faïd. It wasn't me. I'm not guilty. I was waiting for a bus.

—Are you fucking kidding? We saw you running and tossing the bags.

—He repeated: Not me!

After 48 hours in custody, he was brought to the courthouse in Créteil, where the presiding judge found him guilty of armed robbery in connection with gang activity. He was sent to Fresnes, first division. A tough place. We immediately bought everything he'd need: tracksuit, sneakers, shampoo, shower gel and toothbrushes. I brought it all to the prison myself. The screw looked me over:

—Where do you think you are?

None of it was allowed.

We sent money orders for 4000–5000 francs so he could buy goods at the commissary. And we hired Jean-Louis Pelletier as his lawyer. Because, for us, he was the best.*

* Pelletier (b. 1936), a high-profile lawyer, was also favored by the celebrated criminal Jacques Mesrine.

We went about this discreetly. We were champs at compartmentalizing things. We obviously said little to Pelletier, and minimized everything. He offered to get back to us in a week when he'd had a chance to learn more.

And a week later:

— You're screwing with me. The case is very serious!

— We're not really up on the details. What happened?

— Very serious: robbery with unlawful restraint. The BRB is determined to find the other members of the gang... They're furious. You can't even imagine.

In the judge's chambers he'd met with the chief inspector who was leading the inquiry. He and his minions were furious.

They had nothing on us... but I decided to go into hiding.

I started to stay in the Campanile Hotels.* Why? Because at the time they didn't ask for ID. At a local Chamber of Commerce, I'd get the K-bis of some company, then call the hotel, saying I was a sales representative. I'd reserve a room for a week, pay in cash, and use the K-bis to request a bill I could use as a receipt.

So you started learning how to live on the run.

Salespeople are always staying in hotels. You've got to disappear into the crowd.

---

* A European hotel chain.

You drive a little Clio. It's a Renault, the only kind of car you see in the parking lot. You understand these guys wake up at 7:00 AM. At 8:00 AM they go to hustle and come back at 7 or 8 at night. So if you sleep till noon, it looks very fishy. You quickly develop good habits. Up at 7. Breakfast in your room so nobody gets to see too much of your face. Shave and out by 8. Evening, back around 8. These hotels are nicely designed. To get to your room, you don't need to pass the front desk. They're so well laid out that I ended up staying in them for some three years.

As a good salesman, I obviously only stayed there from Monday til Saturday morning. Weekends I always had some place to crash in and around Paris: with a girlfriend or at a friend's place. Monday mornings I'm back in a new Campanile. Every week I'd move from one hotel to another and after a couple of months come back to the first. I never had a problem.

Two months after the episode in Créteil, the fuzz came to search my apartment. When they had him in custody, they caught onto why Fayçal behaved as he did but knew an immediate search & seizure would be useless. They'd probably find nothing. So they opted to wiretap the apartment and watch the comings and goings. In time they knew my whole family. One morning they stormed the place. Afterward, they rounded up everybody: my brother, sister, nephew, even my brother's girlfriend. Who were all totally stunned. My family didn't suspect one-tenth of my activities. For them I was just a high school student, maybe a bit of a schemer, but nothing more. To the point that they were convinced it was a miscarriage of justice. The apartment was totally trashed, everything thrown on the floor. It took days to put things back together. This was all done to apply pressure. *What's with these little Arabs that they fuck with us?* They also picked up two or three of my buddies. Just to kick the anthill...

The three coppers who are on my case, I'm going to get to know well. From a distance. They're completely in the dark; they don't know who they're dealing with. My brother Fayçal was a student with no criminal record, so they figure somebody else was behind him. They were thinking big names and known criminals. I knew cops were tough, and even merciless, but these characters were beyond belief. They handcuffed my sisters to the radiator, insulted my family, and used humiliation in order to make them crack. They're wrong to go after families in that way. They give rise to reactions that you didn't even think possible...

At one point, during interrogation, one of them lashed out:

—You dirty little rats, who do you think you are? You think you're important, in your crappy little Creil housing projects? Think you're gangsters? You're just little shits... I'll show you real criminals.

He brought out photos of three Gauls, from Lyon, of course.

—These are the real gangsters. Big guys. When you're a cop, you catch somebody like that, you can say to yourself, damn, it's the real deal. You — you're nothing but shitty little louts.

This remark got back to me because after each in-terrogation I'd debrief everybody in order to find out whether they'd talked about me.

According to what I've been told, you took revenge. Should I tell you how?

By all means!

You've decided to give the BRB a headache. So first you went to meet the fence, who was surprised to see you.

— You're still at it even after what's happened?

— We keep going. Are you interested or not?

— Yeah, sure.

— So we'll bring you stuff from three jobs.

— What? Three?

— Right. We'll go and do three. Let's go.

He gave you two addresses and you already had a third one picked out but kept it up your sleeve. Out of a desire for revenge and to show what you could do, you planned all three jobs for the same day. One would take place in Évry, another in Paris, and a third in Champs-sur-Marne. Coordination would take you two months.

In Évry, department of L'Essonne, the place is locat-ed in an ordinary industrial zone with parking, so you can simply stay & observe. You've got to ring a bell to get inside the building. Best would be to enter just be-hind somebody. Your target company is on the ground floor and nothing much is happening in another com-pany, on the second floor, so you'll get inside with that company's employees.

For the getaway, you'll have a relay vehicle waiting at a Total gas station off Highway 6. You'll be paying attention to surveillance cameras in the industrial park and gas station, etc. So your stolen automobiles are completely refitted with no signs of being broken into & displaying the proper insurance cards — just to let the cops know who they're dealing with…

The guy who furnishes the stolen vehicles is a 20-year old from the projects, an ace thief, & cars are his specialty. He wakes up nights at 6:00 PM and goes to bed at 9:00 the next morning after having boosted half a dozen. Plus, he provides them on credit so you'll pay for them when you hit pay dirt.

The car picked up at the gas station will be abandoned at a rest stop along Highway A1, where another will be waiting.

That car is the one you'll use for the noon hold-up in Paris, at Porte des Ternes.

In a military equipment supply store, you'll buy bulletproof vests. You pass yourselves off as journalists leaving for Bosnia and claim the insurance company requires them. You ask for a receipt made out to *Le Figaro*. Why that newspaper? Because you've seen *Flic Story* with Jean-Louis Trintignant as Émile Buisson,* the violent criminal who explains to Inspector Borniche:

— Nobody pays attention to anybody reading *Le Figaro*.

You also buy blue zippered painters' overalls, which you can take off quickly. You'll put them on over business

* A 1975 film directed by Jacques Deray.

suits when you rob a company located on the fourth floor of a building with an elevator that opens directly onto the offices where the RAM is stocked. A suitcase on wheels will make your getaway more discreet as you leave to pick up a car waiting in a "deliveries only" spot in the parking lot. Driving to the gas station to get the first vehicle, you'll go on to Creil to drop off the loot from both the morning and noon jobs. And, that same evening, you'll carry out the third robbery wearing those face masks you've used before: Jacques Chirac, Raymond Barre, François Mitterrand. The victims of all three hold-ups will be cuffed with the same Serflex, just so the BRB will have no doubts....

The nighttime robbery is a regular Fort Knox. Security cameras, regular police patrols, location in a highly protected industrial park. The director lives in the town of Gagny while the hold-up is to take place in Champs-sur-Marne.* To enter this place, you'll make a phony delivery of flowers between 7:30–7:45 PM.

To prepare for all three jobs, you rent a meeting room in a Campanile Hotel and, after reviewing the whole plan with visual aids, you'll stay the night.

You purchase a good deal of equipment. In addition to overalls and good quality business suits, you've got walkie-talkies, the very latest earpieces & tie-clip microphones, hairpieces, leather gloves...

For weapons, you've managed to get a submachine gun — an HK MP5 bought from an Albanian. From

---

* The two towns on the outskirts of Paris are located about 7 km apart, or 30 minutes by car.

whom you also ordered an Uzi and four semi-automatic pistols with ammunition.

April 17, 1996 is D-day. Each of you knows his role when you start off about 5:30 AM to avoid rush hour traffic along the *Francilienne*.*

At 7:55 AM you're in Évry and there — surprise: the front door is wide open and somebody's carrying out boxes.

You rush out of the car, hustle the employees inside, and shut the door. Of the five employees, only the director goes for his phone. One of you aims the Uzi at him and orders him to keep calm and open the safes. Once the employees are cuffed, you fill two big bags and take off. You change vehicles and arrive around 9:15 AM in Vémars. A debrief in the gas station's cafeteria and less than two hours later you're off to Place des Ternes. There, you fill just half a bag, but it brings you about 800,000 francs. The first hold-up brought about 1,700,000...

You drive back to Vémars where you toss all the bags into another car that you'll unload in a garage around 3 PM. Two hours later, wearing disguises, you arrive in Gagny at the home of the company's manager.

Bingo: the gate is open and the manager is there with his whole family. You won't be tying them up but will let them spend the night together. The next morning, two of you escort the manager in his car. To keep in touch with your partner, who's watching the family,

---

* The belt highway roughly parallel to the *périphérique* that encircles metropolitan Paris.

you've brought your own telephones for fear of leaving behind traces of DNA.

One of you enters the place with the manager, making clear that when you leave he'll have to be smiling as if nothing has happened. This third and final job will turn out to be the jackpot: worth 3,200,000 francs on the street. In 24 hours, you've made 5,700,000 — almost 900,000 euros.

Two days later, in the article in *France-Soir*, the police underscore your professionalism, with accomplices who address each other by number not name. And no violence.

So, what comes next?

I was 23 years old and already thinking of retiring. A friend who worked at Roissy-Charles-de-Gaulle found me a job as a customer service agent. I discovered I was a talented worker. After three weeks, the manager of the recruitment agency told me:

— I'm hiring you permanently. Thirty of you are still in training, but I'm bringing you on board right away.

He appointed me supervisor of the 1st-class lounge at British Airways, where they needed a male presence. There I'd meet Cantona, David Ginola, Kim Basinger, Luc Besson... Women dug me & the airline's number two executive appreciated the work I was doing. I'd settled down. I had a job, nice apartment, and plenty of money saved. I really thought about stopping. Truly. I'm done.

With everything going well, the only black cloud was my brother, who was locked up. I felt guilty. Why had I let him come along? I've got to take care of his girlfriend & of the family. And then too I'm worried. Aren't the cops going to end up in tracking me down?

BRB investigators are on the case. They're looking into computer crime. One thing led to another, & eventually they got to Marc.

What happened was that, on October 2, 1996, the cops came barging into the house again. This time they had it in for me. Why? Because they'd kept a photo of me that they'd found during the earlier search of the place. When they caught Marc, the fence, they'd showed it to him.

He told them: "That's him! I don't know his real name but his nickname was 'Pixie.'"

That was the nickname of Dragan Stojkovic, the Serbian soccer player known as the Red Star of Belgrade. A real pro with great technique. Friends of mine who were fans called me that. I was good at soccer and made it to first division. So this guy Marc had made millions with us yet gave me up for nothing! He was only accused of buying stolen goods. He risked very little and had nothing to do with the armed robberies. A few months in jail and he would've been out. Yet this prick ratted on me. Which is only to say, during my whole career as a thief, I was always betrayed. To the point where you tell yourself, *banditism* is really a scene to stay away from.

This squealer also talked about the other fence, the Saudi, whose real identity he fortunately didn't know.

In short, now the BRB is after me. It's a problem for these cops that they underestimate the kids from the projects. The culprit can only be Gaulois, must have spent time in the slammer, and is known by some kind of moniker. It couldn't be Rédoine from Creil — that Algerian from that shit *banlieue*. To them we're just scum and they're blind as bats. They don't surveil us or do stakeouts. They just barge in at six in the morning. Sick fucks. If they'd had me under the least surveillance, they would have collared me. I'd been there the afternoon of the day before. After coming by my place, they went to see my brother Larbi, in case I was with him. Then they hit other places, nearly everybody I knew in Creil. But no Rédoine. So they decide to go after my brother Abdeslam. The fence had recognized him, too. Abdeslam was with me once, simply waiting in a bar across the street. He had nothing to do with anything. He was a university student, and political, against all forms of violence. He did everything he could to warn young people, including me, about the dangers of delinquency. Cops persuaded the judge to lock him up. He'd do a year in preventive detention. But Marc the squealer wouldn't do a single day inside even though his involvement with armed robbery was clearly established.

These BRB pigs go crazy. They tell themselves:

— This Rédoine is one lucky son of a bitch!

But it wasn't luck. It's just that they were dealing with an experienced thief. And I was pre-planning my escape. In anticipation of things going south one day, I'd already got hold of fake identity cards.

How?

Simple. Through an illegal immigrant from North Africa. One of my cousins had false papers this guy had made for him when he arrived from Algiers. He was a pro, a magician. His nickname was The Artist.

I also had to have an authentic passport. I didn't lack for friends. I'd ask them to apply for one, then give it to me but not report it as stolen. For identification, they could get around with their *carte d'identité* while I'd have The Artist turn the passport into a counterfeit for me.

On an Algerian passport, when you remove the foil, an ink overlay comes off with it, sometimes together with the words *République Algérienne*. What did this sneaky bastard do? First he put the passport in a freezer to harden the ink. Then, with a hair dryer, he removed the foil and overlay so he could replace the photo with one of me. Then, with enough pressure, the outline of the stamp would reappear. He replaced the ink overlay *&* redrew the words *République Algérienne*. It worked!

In fact, the guy turned out to be an agent with DRS, the Algerian military security, in charge of infiltrating Islamic extremist groups in France.* I learned that only later. He never gave us up because we weren't terrorists. Making fake papers for us worked well for him just as for us, because we gave him a good reputation. He was really good at what he did. The fake went unnoticed.

---

* Département du Renseignement et de la Sécurité (DRS).

He also made me a driver's license with which I could get a *carte d'identité*. And later on, I was able to get an official fake passport with the help of other papers he forged for me, including a birth certificate, rent receipts, & utility bills.

So, with a new identity, you went into hiding?

I'd also asked The Artist to put an Algerian visa on my passport. Then I left for Algeria via Belgium. From Algiers, I called my people in Creil to tell them where I was, that my brother was innocent, and I'd never come back because I understood nothing about what was going on. Two days later I flew Air Algeria to London, then took the Eurostar to Lille. Bruno came to pick me up and I told him:

— It's war. We're going after an armored truck.

The idea came to you just like that?

I'd gone on the lam and had nothing to lose. Besides, I'm going to need a lot of cash. If I can't steal RAM any longer, there's not a million alternatives. Let's kick it into high gear. Armored trucks have been a dream of mine for a long time. The month before, we kept watching *Heat*. The first time we saw it in a theater, it was like getting punched in the fucking face. *That's what we've got to do next!*

But the problem was that we didn't know how. First, it would be best to go after a cash-in-transit depot. That would be more like the hostage-taking jobs we've done before. We threaten the manager and his family at night, then early next morning we go with him to empty out the place. True, this business doesn't look much like a bank or RAM storage place. But how hard can it be? We'll need a welcoming committee — two or three of us to greet the guards as they arrive, one by one, at the depot. We got this info from the newspapers, and also the fact that there's a security guard inside who opens the door for them. Only thing we have to do now is observe how it works.

If you prefer the depots to armored trucks, is that because you've already done this kind of thing?

No.

Here's what I've been told:

Your partner Bruno had a contact who provided cars, license plates, insurance certificates, etc. He was simply helping you out and when you were doing small-time robberies, you'd give him some stolen merchandise to fence.

One day he sets up a meeting at the Triangle, a nightclub in Andilly, in Val-d'Oise. There you meet a contingent of young guys from that early 1970s generation who came out of the projects to start dealing hashish and doing armed robberies. They were all there with their girlfriends. Most were Arab, some black. Two or three Gauls. All these gangsters from neuf-trois,*

---

* Colloquial reference to the department of Seine-St. Denis, situated to the northeast of Paris, which includes some of the poorest and most disaffected banlieues of Ile-de-France.

Val-d'Oise, and Haut-de-Seine, would meet there. It made you afraid, just coming into the parking lot. There was no GIR* at the time, so as soon as guys like this came into real money, they bought luxury cars, the latest Mercedes, BMWs, Porsches.

The nightclub was managed by a big name in organized crime, Mohammed A., a pioneer *beur*,† well respected around town. You were astonished to see a beur at the top. Just like the police and the press, you thought big gangsters all had names like Jean-Pierre Lepape and Émile Dieudonné.

The guy you were supposed to meet was in fact a Gaul. He would plug you guys into some kind of heist:

— I've been telling people about you. Interested?

— Sure. Why not? But what do they want?

— Some guys want to know about getaway strategies around where you are.

You agreed and went with the guy to show him.

— See this traffic circle? It fills up with gendarmes when they set up a *Plan Épervier*, etc.

What the guy really wants is for you to come aboard because he needs one or two more guys. Until now they're just five. Who was this guy? He was big, a real kingpin of armed robbery. He'd carried out some of the

---

* Groupes d'interventions régionnaux (GIR), created by Nicolas Sarkozy in 2002, when the future president was Minister of the Interior, were designed to attack the underground economy and go after major drug kingpins. [Note by Jérôme Pierrat.]

† *Beur*, or *rebeu*, is Verlan for *Arabe* (French for Arabic or Arab) and designates European-born people whose grandparents are North African immigrants, or specifically Maghreb.

most spectacular attacks on armored trucks during the 1980s. He got out of prison not long ago and wants to get back to robbery. His latest heist was a superb job worth 20,000,000 francs with other criminals from the Parisian underworld. He suddenly blurts out:

— Listen. I just got away with 500 gold ingots. But this year I've got to have twenty million — in cash.

He was wracking his brains trying to plan a job using explosives to blast open the walls of a cash depot. And one of your buddies had advised him to do it instead by using a heavy truck, as the best way to break down the walls. The guy had listened and was smart enough to agree. By the way, he admired you somewhat. He appreciated the fact that, though you were young, you understood the profession. He and his partners were in their 40s, from all over France, and every one of them a Gaul.

So the job went down largely successfully, the money taken.

After that, one of them took you aside:

— You'll go far, but I'm going to give you some advice. Trust nobody. But nobody.

At the time you couldn't understand that. But this guy had spent years in prison, and he'd been held in solitary confinement. He'd been betrayed.

Now back to your cash depot. How did you find it?

At the time, thanks to *Minitel*.* You had only to enter "Brinks" or "Ardial" or "ACDS" in the yellow

---

* A 1980s telephone-based service that provided information about people, places, and businesses throughout France.

pages to bring up the addresses. We started checking them out and tracking them down.

Because it was November and we were going to be spending a lot of time outdoors, we got ready for the cold. We bought ponchos in military surplus stores, snow boots, gloves, ski masks, fleece jackets. Tape recorders for notes and comments. A video camera to film the depot. Also walkie-talkies with earpieces, into which we installed a chip that could lock the person-to-person network and block access. Super-equipped, we drove there for a stake-out in a Renault Express. Except then we realized that these assholes opened their doors at 5:30 in the morning. To be there at 4:30 AM we had to wake up at 3:00.

Morning after morning, we watched how it worked. The first drivers arrived about the same time in three or four different vehicles. The first would enter the code before the three others joined him. A few minutes later, an armored vehicle would come out with the guards aboard, and park in front of the depot.

What would they be waiting for?

A guy in a car. When he arrived, if the armored truck wasn't parked outside, it meant the security procedure had not been carried out, and that could mean criminals waiting inside. In that case, the guy doesn't go inside but leaves instead. One time, the armored vehicle wasn't there, so he turned on a fucking dime. He got paranoid and took off.

Watching that maneuver, we understood that he must be the one with the keys to the vaults. He would arrive around 6:00–6:05 AM and leave immediately afterward. One morning, we even saw him drive up still in his pajamas and bathrobe. He'd come out of bed just to open the door to the vaults before going back home.

In the end we got to know all the guards and gave each a nickname: Mustache, Baldy, Fatso, Babar, Jean Carmet.

We noted everything: each car make and model, plate number, and so on. But we were particularly interested in the guy with the key to the vaults.

To know where he lived, we had to follow him. Because for this job, we couldn't use the K-bis attack. We decided to tail him with four cars, the way the police operate. Each car was equipped with a walkie-talkie. I'd already practiced this method for the jewelry store robbery, but my accomplices on this job hadn't. So, to teach them, it was back to the *périphérique* where we practiced whole days following cars. We became wildly good at it. But, to be a good tail, you have to know the territory inside out, and we realize that Paris is a dangerous place for us — the cops are at home there and know all the streets. Not us. Conclusion: don't drive in Paris, take the subway. That puts the cops in our territory because we were taking the RER to Châtelet-les-Halles in the center of Paris since we were 12 years old.

Finally, we figure out where the guy lives, but we're far from a solution. We've also got to neutralize the guard who silences the alarm in the morning.

And even if we take their families hostage, he and the controller have to interact with the others but they can't be able to talk. So we decide to wrap explosives around their waists. But we don't have explosives. So we'll use modeling clay wrapped in adhesive tape.

— *If you do anything stupid, it'll take a fucking steam shovel to dig you out. Because we'll blow you to smithereens from a distance. Got that?*

To apply pressure, the families won't be at home but held in a van 30 miles away.

Two families to hold hostage, so two guys to escort them. A welcoming committee to greet the guards when they arrive in the morning, with one guy outside to warn us if somebody else arrives. Three more to empty the vaults.

That makes eleven! Bruno tells me: "Shit! It's like a soccer team." We're just four.

Now it's late January, and the planning phase has taken three months.

And in the end it came to nothing.

Watching the depot gave us a good understanding of how this armored truck business worked. Schedules, routes — we learned it all. We knew the guards, what they looked like up close. We pretended to be hitchhikers to memorize their faces and practice profiling. We knew them, from the mechanic's shaved head to the old guys ready to retire.

Before long the idea took shape: what if we simply robbed an armored truck instead of the depot.

Yes, but you lack crucial information. How much money was in the truck?

Without some kind of informant inside, it's very difficult to know when trucks leave the depot. However, it's easier to guess the amount in trucks coming back. We watched the supermarket near the depot and knew that when they picked up cash there, they'd have collected about 1,000,000 francs.* The problem was that not all the armored trucks were from the same depot. So we kept track of plate numbers. Sometimes it didn't matter because we recognized the drivers.

So we finally chose our target. But where to carry out the attack? At the point when the truck returns to the depot. Why fuck around in a supermarket parking lot or someplace along the open highway? Near the depot, a group of thieves can ambush it with the help of a lookout strategically located near where the truck has to pass. Which raises the next question: how to stop the truck?

Little by little we worked out the technique to corner & capture — the ambush. We had time to figure it out, which is the advantage of living on the lam. Time is on your side; you don't have to deal with the little things of life. This is what you do. You live in a bubble.

To rob an armored truck, you've got to set yourself up like a military organization. It's not like the classic bank holdup or robbing an ATM. It's a war movie.

* Approximately 50,000 euros.

You're going to be confronting armed guys in bulletproof vests. They'll be armor-plate protected and meeting you with pump-action shotguns. To launch the assault, you've got to have military capability and damned good warriors.

If they're warriors, that means they've got to be ready to shoot…

No, we'll do everything to avoid that. We're constantly concerned about casualties. No wounded, no innocent victims. In a case like this, that means setting the bar very high. If you want to go after an armored truck, that means stopping it, aiming guns at the guards, taking them out of the truck, cuffing them. No pistol-whipping, no vulgar language. Otherwise, things can fall apart. We're going to take the money and go. We know we can do it. Because we've got the experience, have been through it before, and because we've had results. What's key is you've got to think and take your time.

We check out the place on Sundays, when the depot is closed. You don't risk coming across a guard in street clothes. We walk around to soak up the surroundings: *this no good but here might work, it's calm and we can get away fast*. We've been coming every day, so by now we know the place inside out — the roads, the times you'll have traffic jams, the places where cops will set up roadblocks… We know this area better than where we live; we've spent hours and whole evenings here. And that's very important because the second crucial point when you attack an armored truck is the getaway.

Immobilization of the truck is 60-70% of the job and the most difficult phase of the operation. Only serious professionals can properly stop an armored truck. Blocking and stopping a behemoth like this, which weighs six tons, to ambush it before the guards even realize what's happened, to take possession of the space around the truck during the entire four to five minutes of the attack, and to control and restrain passersby as well as the guards, while at the same time you're holding everything down — that's not something just anybody can pull off.

With the armored truck, if you leave an opening of a single inch, it will barrel through and be gone. It's built like an assault tank. It can smash cars. When it wants to get away, it will run right over you. And if the driver decides to try to escape, his colleagues will all but sprout wings alongside him. It's like: *They want trouble, we'll give them trouble. Ready, aim, fire.* So it's crucial to stop the truck cold, in a way that's totally clear and precise.

We thought of using a traffic spike. Why? Because in 1995 some guys had used it to rob a Brinks truck in the north, around Lesquin. It seems they were Belgians from a tough neighborhood in Brussels. These wise guys laid down a spike strip at night. When the truck was on its way back home at 11:00 AM, the driver didn't see it in the dark. The thieves had to stop the truck by running it down. But the truck kept going even with flat tires. Then when the thieves went to work, the guards refused to open the doors. So they blasted off some dynamite that killed them.

A bloody armed robbery, Belgian style. They're very violent, the Belgians. You'll never see an attack on an armored truck in Belgium without shooting and casualties. Naturally, even if they got away with 15,000,000 francs, we weren't going to take them as examples. But from any attack on an armored truck, you can take away something positive. In this case, it was the spike strip. Except we wouldn't be attacking in dark of night. It's spring now and they'd see it. We thought of painting the spike tar-gray but that was too risky and likely wouldn't be effective.

We then considered blocking the vehicle with a pair of trucks, one in front and the other behind. But that would require extreme technique & tremendous synchronization.

We knew full well this wasn't a game. You risk your life and you're going to be risking that of others. We're not going to be chased by traffic cops, and the prison sentences we're looking at aren't speeding tickets. We're entering another world. We began as bandits and became capable thieves, but now we're in the championship league.

At the time, some seven or eight years had gone by without attacks on armored trucks in and around Paris. Big gangs from the southern suburbs, from Montreuil, and guys from the Dream Team,* who'd

---

* A gang that perpetrated a series of dramatic thefts beginning in the 1990s, first in France and later in Spain, which adopted the nickname for the 1992 United States men's Olympic basketball team.

already hit depots, had tried armored trucks without success. Discipline was the motto of gangs from the south, from Corsica and Marseilles.

We faced a fucking challenge. The guards we targeted were particularly devious and cunning: in 1995, attacked by some guys from Montreuil and the southern banlieue, they'd refused to open up. One thief was wounded. Same deal in 1996 with guys from the Dream Team who'd stopped the vehicle with two concrete mixer trucks, one in front, the other behind. Again the guards refused to open the door. One of them even had a cardiac arrest. And during another attack in 1997, one of the outlaws got killed.

A priori, these guys weren't going to open the door. We had to show from the very first second that this was no laughing matter. Bluff or no bluff, they had to be scared out of their fucking wits. We had to make them piss themselves. We had to convince them that the only way out alive would be to open the door. To dream up the best way to do that, we rented a conference room in a motel. On the blackboard we drew an armored truck with its front and side kill holes. At this point I noticed something: the driver's side has three kill holes and one kill hole front and back. On each side, a lateral door. Because they never know on which side they're going to load or unload, that spares them making a U-turn. They can open the truck faster.

We won't attack from the side, where they can aim and shoot in three directions. Rather, we'll come at them head-on.

If you make the right decision at the start, everything else automatically falls into place. Pretty much like in a video game: you make the right move and further solutions come easily. First of all, with this approach, two of the three guards will be helpless. They won't be able to aim their three guns out the narrow kill holes. Second, you can see what the three guys are doing — for example, if they're reaching for their .357 Magnums. Attacking from the side, it's not the same. The truck rides high and they can duck down. And third, you can see if they're petrified & panicked.

Last but not least, you must never fire on an armored vehicle. The guards' reflex is to crouch down & take up arms to defend themselves. Worse, you're giving them courage and the strength to fight back.

We debate the issues. Everybody says what he thinks. And we reach an agreement. From this first meeting we realize we're figuring out how to proceed. Just like the jobs with RAM or other kinds of hits, we take the thing seriously and get to the place we want to be. You must understand, we're talking psychology of the outlaw. There are three or four of us, and we're thinking about it day and night. We eat sleep and dream armored truck. We talk about it when we drive; we're totally into it. It's an extraordinary process. We take three or four months to plan a job that goes down in three or four minutes. You can imagine what sort of state we'll be in at the moment of attack. Mentally and psychologically, we'll be in better shape than they are. We're charged up, fully engaged, we've got courage and we're ready to go.

Aren't you scared?

Whoever tells you he's not scared is either crazy or a liar. You start to be afraid as soon as you start preparing. Because you know it's going to be serious. Closer you get to the act itself, the more you feel the pressure. It's extremely nerve-racking. Fear is a sensation. Gangsters are just like cops, they seek it out, push it to the limit. When you rob an armored truck, your adrenaline shoots up. It hits a peak. You know you're putting your life on the line. You're going to confront three well-trained armed guards protected by tank-grade armor-plating. It requires a high degree of concentration. Your positioning and the moves you make must be very precise. Nobody talks; you read each other by eye contact. You hear your heart beat strong and fast. It's the middle of winter but you're drowning in sweat. Your blood freezes in your veins. Gazes go ice cold. Then suddenly — it starts! At this point you don't hear anything. It's war. The earth stops turning. You're in another dimension. Total immersion. Not too relaxed, but superfocused. You're into it — and then you're done. It's over. Back home that night, you're drained. You still feel the heart palpitations as you're falling asleep.

If all this puts you into such a terrible state, why do it?

Your question makes me uneasy. I can't tell you. It's hard to find a really good answer. You commit an armed robbery, face-to-face against guys with weapons.

Not only can they shoot you but, what's more, you've got to neutralize them without hurting anybody. You've got to stand up to them. Does that make me crazy or what? It takes you to the fine line between reason & insanity. We're right in between, because we're launching the attack in a technical manner. We calculate and weigh the risks. But listen, when you go through such an emotional storm and come out alive after pulling it off, you end up feeling *ecstatic*. Later you'll have to think it through completely because you've got to get ready to get right back in the game.

Let's get back to the affair at hand, you still have to refine it.

Day after day, from observation. For example, we spot an armored truck parked in the street. And what do we see? A guard smoking a cigarette and ashing through the kill hole. We cross the street in front of the truck without looking at him. A look that's even a bit too focused could be deadly! They're very suspicious. Because he's slivered opened the kill hole, you get to see a little bit inside and realize that their room for maneuver is not even 10 centimeters. That means he can't get his hand out the kill hole but only the barrel of his gun, and he can't move it laterally. So, the closer you get, the less his ability to aim. If you plaster yourself to the side of the truck, you're out of range. You've just realized they can't touch you. Quite something.

You've got the technical part down, but now you need military-grade weapons.

We've got to have assault rifles. Without them, we'll look like amateurs. But even that won't be enough to make them open the door. They'll feel safe knowing that bullets can't penetrate the armor-plated truck.

We think of brandishing a rocket-launcher to freak them out but in fact we won't need one. Why? Because there's a new recruit. A guy we met in Israel.

Only in the projects could you see this kind of thing. Big name gangsters would meet one another in the prison yard or in bars and nightclubs. We were considered maybe thugs and armed robbers but in no way did we belong to that world of grand larceny. That was not how we met people. We didn't mingle or hang out in nightclubs. However, we did spend time in video game rooms. And one day in one of them, in Tel Aviv, a guy heard us speaking French.

— So you're French? Me too. I'm doing my *Aliya.*[*]

It was almost touching to see a guy who'd left France hoping to find paradise in Israel. Most people travel to Israel only on vacation. Two or three weeks in Tel Aviv, time on the beach and a meal at the Old Man and the Sea, a good restaurant where the French always meet to order schnitzel and falafels. They sunbathe, stroll through Tel Aviv, visit the Wailing Wall in Jerusalem, and go to nightclubs. Two weeks in Israel is wonderful. But daily life is less pleasant.

[*]   Ritual immigration to Israel.

Wages are far lower than in France: you work harder to earn less. You come with diplomas? They're a dime a dozen. Life is expensive and you suffer. More misery: you miss your family. I've known any number of French Jews like that, who couldn't hold out a year — but others who emigrate with their children and whole families, leaving everything behind to settle in Israel permanently.

Bruno *&* Stéphane *&* I, we admired those people. They'd said fuck it and left it all for Israel! When we met this guy, we thought he was like them. Wrong. If he was gone for good, it was because his parents didn't want him in France. They saw things were going to end badly. And effectively, that was why we got along from the start. We spoke the same language. He had our number, too. He spent time with us and since he didn't have much money, we paid for restaurants and entertainment. Here was a good guy, we realized, even if he's a little mental. If you're with your girlfriend, he won't even look at her. He's respectful. And when you ask him:

— What do you do for living?
— I'm in the military.
— What the fuck! And what do you do in there, bro?
— Civil engineer.

He couldn't have fallen among better friends. We were crazy about weapons. When we see soldiers in the streets, we're like little kids.

— Look at that M16! That Galil! Look at those — they're rocket-launchers!

So one day the guy brings around his M16. In Israel, it's very common to see a soldier with his rifle.

He took us to a field and gave us a box of ammunition. We started spending whole half days shooting. Some 15 kilometers north of Tel Aviv, among the orange groves, we targeted the fruit on the trees. The third time we went, we ran into a guard. He just thought we were crazy. The country is full of deserted areas, so we just found another place to shoot. The only thing we were afraid of was a military helicopter. But later, we stopped going into the countryside. For 150 euros, we could do it legally at firing ranges.

We went to Eilat, where a retired Israeli army officer who'd fought in the Six Day War taught us how to shoot. Everything from the Galil to the Jericho pistol, the Uzi to the M16. We spent whole days there learning how to shoot and handle firearms.

At his apartment, our new friend showed us how to disassemble & reassemble an M16. He explained the various types of bullets, from tracers to dumdums and blanks. Everything. The result? We became both gun connoisseurs and really good marksmen.

Did you discuss crime with your new friend?

He didn't say anything but we knew he'd been hanging out with Russians who committed petty crimes, break-ins, that kind of thing. In Israel it was like the 1930s. To rob a convenience store, all you had to do was climb onto the roof, break in, and take what you wanted. There were no armed robberies in Israel at the time. The big thing was stealing cars. Mostly done by Arabs.

Arabs and Jews, in terms of the thief-ocracy, worked hand in hand, and it's too bad that in politics they don't find a way to get along just as well! Even politicians got into debating why the Israeli and Palestinian mafias got along like brothers.

At the time, there was good business in stolen cars, but few robberies. The first time I changed money at a foreign currency exchange, I almost died laughing. There was no airlock and only one guy manned the office. Behind him was a vault filled with 300,000 dollars. Our only problem was the old saw about how you better not shit where you eat. Which is a little simplistic for my taste. All the more since they dealt only in cash, and a lot of it. We were impressed. We could have pulled off a nice job. And sometimes we got itchy. But we weren't completely stupid and knew that we'd better not get noticed.

Did you let your friend know who you were?

One day, we started to. He asked if we'd like guns of our own. He didn't know what we did for a living but noticed we paid for everything in cash. So we told him out of the blue that we were thieves and to make things clear I added, for myself, I wasn't a feuj but a rebeu.

"No kidding! You know what? I thought all three of you were Arabs."

Did your buddy supply you with guns?

Even better. Talking with him, we realized he was an expert in explosives.

Meantime, back in France we did some reconnaissance and returned to Israel for a couple of weeks, just to relax in Tel Aviv. This time we did need somebody like him for a big job. He didn't seem surprised.

— What's it about?

— An armored truck.

He immediately agreed. Together we went to observe how the armored trucks operated in Tel Aviv. They had only two guards and were built like trash cans. He told us he could blow them open very easily. We showed him photos we'd brought from France. Those models wouldn't pose a problem, either.

But he had to find explosives. A couple of days later, he brought back several kilos he'd stolen from a soldier who guarded army tanks. Each of which carried a stock of plastic explosives, smoke grenades, and a survival kit. He'd succeeded in getting them by diverting his buddy's attention. We learned the difference between an electrical detonator, a fused detonator, and one with a percussion cap. In Israel, they have the most sophisticated equipment.

In empty fields we practiced how to handle the detonators. Our friend explained that the material is delicate and accidents are frequent. He was a perfectionist who acted like an instructor in the *Tazhal*.*

---

* The acronym for the Israeli Defense Force (IDF).

He was a virtuoso. He worked as a mine clearing expert: he cleared the ground for commandos and then covered them with his M16 from a sniper's post as they passed through.

Our training included handling C4, penthrite, Semtex... After becoming good marksmen, now we were explosives experts.

Ok, but you didn't have this kind of material in France...

Right, it was no small problem: how to bring this stuff into France. Out of the question to take it on a plane. So we thought of a Jewish buddy who often traveled to Israel. He knows about our schemes and stuff but was himself straight. Every gangster needs to know somebody honest who has a place where he can sleep or leave papers and things.

For me, he was a friend from childhood who always helped out when I was in trouble.

And this guy smuggled three detonators that he hid on himself. He had to be very careful because at the time, the Israeli customs officers used a type of glove that reacts to explosive substances; they'd pat you down or pass it across the luggage. So we laminated the detonators to avoid any emanation. We were equally afraid of the explosive detection dogs. We used hair spray to cover a kilo of plastic explosive that the guy smuggled through accompanied by his wife and children. He got a handsome reward!

However, with an assault weapon, it's impossible. For that we had to go underground.

I decided to go through the fence who'd promised to buy the merchandise from the jewelry heist in Chantilly. He was a big name, a beur from the projects in the 93rd.* He was dependable *&* managed his team of five guys with an iron fist. He was a genuine "Scarface" from the projects. He earned 500,000 euros each month by reselling 500 kilos of hashish to well-known and established thugs from the southern *banlieues,* who showed him considerable respect. In the early 1990s, many of these guys were just out of prison for armed robbery and so they turned to drug dealing.

I'd met this fence through a semi-wholesaler in Creil he was supplying and with whom I got along right away. This guy had quickly sized me up *&* knew I was serious. He so often had to deal with fuckups, people who were always late. He was a professional. Like me, he drove a rented car, woke up at 5:00 in the morning, and ended his days at 11:00 at night. When I needed little things like license plates and insurance certificates, I'd go to him. And I did little things for him in return. He was my age, 24, and we got along really well. Even if I wasn't drawn to that scene, I've got to say the guy deserved my respect. At the head of a gang that was more or less family, he took good care of his business, never squealed, served as top guy in his *banlieue.* He controlled a large sector of the 93rd.

---

* The *neuf-trois,* in plain speech, refers to administrative department 93, located northeast of Paris. Its population is largely impoverished. See also p. 99.

Let's back up: tell me about the fence.

The fence himself was this great big felon from a project, a guy involved in all kinds of stuff. He followed the money. He was a wholesaler, to be sure, but also a fence. He could pay cash for Lacoste goods, buy your truckload of whisky or Moroccan rugs.

This was the guy I went to see for the Kalashnikovs. They were just then coming into France and there weren't many. But no problem, he'll find them for me. Despite the fact he was fed up with supplying arms mainly to old-fashioned gangsters who were just as often phonies who'd put in orders for them but then not buy, so he'd lose cred. He knew he wouldn't have that problem with me. He searched here and there, and laid hands on two Kalashnikovs and a single Uzi, bought from dealers he knew — guys from the neighborhood who got them through an Albanian who was smuggling them in small quantities.

Now that we had assault weapons, we needed bulletproof vests. We went to a Parisian military supply store where we pretended to be journalists leaving to cover a war... We reinforced the vests with leather pockets that we'd read about in a book on the GIGN. For combat gear, it was easy: military supply store. Balaclavas? Motorcycle shops. Equestrian and golf gloves: we bought them at Décathlon. At a place in Rosny-sous-Bois we posed as owners of a security firm and bought Kenwood walkie-talkies that we could lock on five frequencies. We added tie-clip microphones & ear receivers. We prepared like commandos.

And you've got a precise target?

Totally precise, because we're going to get help from a mole in the armored transportation company. Every armed robber's dream!

My friend the drug dealer in Creil told me about him. The guy bought hashish for himself, and happened to confide where he was working. I said that I'd like to meet him. No problem. He introduced me and the guy in fact worked at the depot itself, and didn't seem fazed when I tell him what I've got in mind. He didn't ask anything about what I'd been doing but seemed concerned only about the method we were planning to use to stop the truck. I immediately reassure him that we won't be doing any shooting. I explain in detail the idea about the kill holes:

— No matter. If you threaten us at gunpoint, he tells me, we'll get out of the truck. There are no heroes in this company.

So then we study possible lines of attack. A big convoy travels from the depot at Arcueil in Val-de-Marne to the depot in Villepinte. There they load and unload cash, about 100,000,000 francs, or more than 15,000,000 euros. That works for me.

And I know Villepinte. We've already surveilled the depot there. But we were bothered by the police station located nearby, just a couple hundred feet away. Our mole comes back with details. The armored truck takes one of two routes, and it's the driver's decision. But at all events, he'll arrive at Villepinte. So that's where we'll attack.

Our guy will give me the number of the truck at 7:00 PM the day of the attack, to be sure we've got the right one. Okay. But I won't be able to use a phone on site because the cops could trace the wireless access point and discover where the call came from. Instead, he'll call the number of a phone booth in Paris where somebody will answer and then call me.

The next Thursday we move on to surveillance. We saw the problems that could arise if two Brinks trucks both appeared at the same time, especially if one of them was a "tank"— an oversize armored model about one-and-a-half times as large as the regular ones, equipped with tinted windows that prevent you from seeing inside. If that's the truck, we will put off the job for a week.

As the reconnoitering continues, I start to figure out the right place for the attack. At the exit off A86, the Brinks passes around a traffic circle that gives onto a six-lane avenue before turning left into the driveway that leads to the depot, which is situated in a small industrial zone. We won't be able to attack in the traffic circle; it's too busy and not far from the police station. The avenue itself is so wide that the truck could escape. But the driveway is perfect. It's deserted and the driver won't see it coming. To bring the Brinks to a stop, we'll exploit a defect.

Steel plates protect the back wheels but not the front ones, because they have to be able to turn. So we'll strike the front wheels. We'll bring out the guards, cuff them, take the money and leave.

We discuss the possible arrival of the cops but we're not worried at all about the depot or about the 30 armed guards who work there. They don't impress us at all, even though we're going to be attacking their co-workers just under their noses.

Bruno will be posted in front of the depot with his assault rifle and a rocket launcher on his back. We'll see if anybody moves! I doubt they'll come outside because we're in a position to welcome them with the barrel of a gun. The depot had one defect — there was only a single entrance. All you had to do was watch that and nobody could get out.

Our driver, though, seems a little hesitant when it comes to stopping the Brinks. Will this technique work or not? So I will be in charge of driving the vehicle. I'll turn sharply left at the very last moment and break the wheel of the truck.

The police station in Villepinte needs further thought. I drive there in my little Clio, arriving about 11:00 AM. I buy a sandwich and sit down on one of the little benches in front of the police station. I see the paddy wagons, the little patrol vehicles, and watch the passing plainclothesmen of the BAC* in their Peugeot 306s. I get back in my car and note that driving between the police station and our location

* Officers of the anti-crime brigade.

takes just one minute. The police will be getting a call within 15 seconds after the attack begins, and they'll have a little discussion:

— *What's happening?*

— *Armored vehicle under attack!*

...That's going to take maybe 30 seconds. Now it's been 45 seconds. They'll be responding in a group of at least three or four. And what will it be like for the cop in the police station? He won't be wearing his pistol — or there'll be at least one who's not. He'll have to go fetch it, maybe even load it. He'll also have to put on his bulletproof vest, which at the time was optional. They're going to waste some time. Now we've gone past three minutes fifteen seconds. Plus the minute to drive that I timed in the car. So let's say four minutes in all.

We think that we can pull off the hit in three minutes and thirty seconds. I'm sure the guards will open up for us without a problem.

That perplexes the others.

— Wait a minute. What makes you so sure?

— Not sure? Who'd have the balls to attack an armored truck a couple hundred feet from a police station?

So then we go to work on the getaway route. We've got to avoid passing the police station. At the wheel of my little Clio, I figure out a plan. An overhead bridge crosses over highway A104. It leads to Roissy nearby. Which is fantastic. We'll change cars at the airport because, as we saw from the film *Heat,* helicopters are not allowed to fly over airports.

Because this was your first such attack, tell us a little about the stress & anxiety.

Tension rises during practice simulations. Over days before the heist, we carried out the same moves over and over. These were training exercises. In the heat of the moment, we won't have to think, we'll be on automatic.

We time everything. How much time do we have to get the guards out? 30 seconds. How long will it take to tie them up? 30 seconds? We've got to be able to do it in half that, which adds up to 45 seconds. The guy who goes into the truck to empty the bags, how much time does he need? As soon as we get the guards out, we've got to get inside. Et cetera.

Are you afraid?

Yes. You perceive the fear in others. Even if they try not to show it, you see it in their eyes. But tremendous determination energizes us all. To rob an armored truck, it's absolutely key — more powerful than the explosives or the assault rifles or anything else. It's a case of *de-ter-mi-na-tion*. We're physically and mentally conditioned. We're at the top of our game. We've also got solid experience. We've got the calm self-control of professionals. But in addition, we like the job. There's no hostage-taking, it doesn't go on all night, just four minutes. It'll be a great heist!

I propose we wear hockey masks to really scare the guards.

— Stop your bullshit, Doc!

— No. We'll wear masks. Like in *Heat,* we'll scare the bejesus out of them.

Over the next couple of days, we receive the masks by courier. If this works, we'll keep using them; they'll become our signature. Not to preen or stick it to the world like the clever Postiches gang;[*] we only wanted the guards to know who they were dealing with. If the attack comes off well, the next victims will think: "These guys aren't going to kill us. Just open the door. They're professionals, no joke."

We also have to deal with the vehicles. The one we'll use to plow into the Brinks will certainly get damaged, so we'll leave it on the spot. We also need two small vans to block it, front and back. You never know but, even with a broken wheel, they could still play the hero and try to take off. We'll also have another car, stationed at the traffic circle in Villepinte, to signal when the Brinks is coming. That makes four so far. We'll escape in two cars and have two more parked at the airport. That makes eight altogether. I've got a professional car thief working with me. He's already got a Renault Safrane and an Audi. For myself I've already two Renault Expresses. The others, including the two trucks, I order through a car thief in Creil.

I do a final inventory of all equipment, then on Thursday a final investigation of the place.

I avoid delegating tasks. I do everything myself. That prevents four or five guys from screwing up.

---

[*] The Gang des Postiches operated in the early 1980s and carried out more than two dozen bank robberies in and around Paris.

Then you're almost ready?

Except we still don't know how many we should be. For the answer we call on our Professor, Michael Mann. In *Heat* he goes with five, so we're missing two. The fence from the 93rd found them for me — a beur and his friend, a Malian from Drancy. Both seem cool. These are guys from the projects, but not like us. They're always going to nightclubs, shooting cocaine, hanging out with so-called big gangsters. In a word, they're hoodlums.

They talk slang. One of them would ask:
— Want to meet in a *rade*?
— What's that? I ask. Tell me.
— A bar.
The guy almost makes me feel like a peasant.
— You know my *papelard*?
— Your wallet?
— No, my resume.
Who is this dingbat? We decide we'll keep him for one or two jobs, after that he's out of here. Get rid of him, drop kick him back to the projects.

As to the beur, he's on the lam. He's just come from Marbella, broke and practically a *clochard*. There he hung out with thugs. He's a guy who dreams of being a gangster who lives by gangsta rules. At this point, we don't see him as a little shit. Rather, he's ballsy. He's got some equipment — a .38 special and one grenade. He arrives with his friend, who wants to sell us an AK-47 for 25,000 francs. Here's a guy who's going to rob an armored truck and meanwhile wants to scam us when we've already spent 100,000 francs on him. But the fence convinced me:

— Go ahead, it's tough as shit to find these guns. Buy it. So I do.

It's risky to set up this kind of job with strangers.

I've got the feeling that the beur is not a pro, even if he's already been into robbing banks. Maybe he'd showed some ability to lead when he was with his minions in the 93rd. On this job he's just a soldier but eager to do it and seems feisty. I prefer him to a slug.

The problem, however, is that my friends don't like the two newcomers. Something doesn't click. For myself, I don't get those bad vibes.

But the other guy turns out to have a big mouth. We didn't know that yet. After the job's over, the drug dealer from the 93rd would tell me:

— Be careful, he shoots too much coke and jabbers a lot. He's bought himself a motorbike. And now everybody knows he's done Brinks. Be careful.

— Well, *shit*.

— Don't worry. He doesn't know your name.

What we didn't know is that the beur acts the same. He tells his life story to anybody who'll listen. He says now he's rolling with top thieves. He brags:

— It's me, I'm in on armored truck robberies. I'm one of the hockey players — that's me. I'm top of the heap.

He thinks he's somebody. Of course, my friends had warned me:

— These guys aren't like us.

That was true. They didn't live clean like us. They were overconfident. They were always laughing and making jokes. Which is not at all my friends' thing, if you know what I mean.

To stay safe, we have as little to do with them as possible. We don't want to fall into some kind of trap laid by the GIGN or the RAID.* The armed robber's number one enemy is ambush by the pigs. So to the two guys I'd said nothing except:

— We've got a job coming up. You might be interested.

So everything's ready. How long before the attack?

A few days. I decide to go to Cannes to relax. We booked rooms at the Carlton. I rest, swim in the pool or go to the beach. I clear my head. Despite meticulous planning, I'm still filled with doubts. I can't stop questioning myself. I keep wondering if it's going to work, if I'm right, if I haven't forgotten something.

You risk your life in this business. I'm putting other people's lives at risk, too, and I never forget that guns can talk. You're going to be dealing with guards bearing shotguns and .357 Magnums. And when the cops arrive, they're not going to be shouting "Hands up!" You're wearing bulletproof vests and armed with assault rifles. It's clear they won't have second thoughts. They'll draw their guns and empty their mags.

* For GIGN, see p. 44. RAID (*Recherche, Assistance, Intervention, Dissuasion*) is similarly an elite tactical police unit.

So what the fuck — I'm down for it. I'm 24 years old.
— *This hit's too good. We're going to beat the shit out of them.*

I'm fired up and get back to Paris. Our cars are ready, all with license plates registered to the 93rd — I congratulate the kids. Again we rent a conference room at the Campanile and learn our parts by heart. We sketch a picture of the Brinks truck. Each of us knows where to go and what to do. Before leaving, we decide to meet on Wednesday, the day before the attack.

A final rehearsal takes place in the woods. It's loud and fast. I rack my brains thinking through our plan to immobilize the vehicle. It's absolutely up to me to bring it to a stop. Because I'm the one who's going to slam into the front wheels.

— Don't worry, I tell them. But when I'll stop the thing, the air bag may blow up in my face, I'll be stuck. You'll have to come get me. Otherwise they'll shoot me.

I'll make sure to have a switchblade with me to burst the air bag if need be. I'll be driving the Safrane, a sturdy car that won't crumple and crush me if the impact is too great. It's the V6 model with fuel injection so, powerful enough to break the axle. It's new, with just a few thousand miles on it. My friend broke it in on the *peripherique*.

The second issue is execution speed. We've got to make precise gestures that get the guards out within 5 to 10 seconds. Ten seconds lost, that's three police cars on the scene. Ten seconds gained, that's one less confrontation with the cops.

When D-Day arrives, we must make a change to our meticulous plan. The parents of the person at whose place we'd intended to meet after the hit have unexpectedly returned home from vacation. So we have to take two connecting rooms at the Campanile in Senlis. Most important, we can enter without passing the reception desk. Moreover, no guard, camera, or code.

We get ready. Does everybody have his equipment? Overalls, balaclava, hockey mask, bulletproof vest with walkie-talkie hooked up and connected to the micro-tie, grenades, a Beretta 9 mm as backup if the automatic pistol jams, and an assault rifle with four or five cartridges, grenades, all of it. In addition, we have a heavy MG-42 machine gun to impress the guards, and a rocket launcher. We have Uzi pistols stashed in the door compartments, should a problem arise. I'm carrying an M16 with a folding grip and, just in case, a .357 Magnum on my back in a backpack.

We've got to be on site and ready that evening at 7:30–7:45.

And when it's time?

We all arrive in the van. The cars are already in place, everybody has a key slipped inside one of his gloves. We're wearing the overalls and it's a hot day in July. We're sweating like pigs in this little fucking Peugeot. With the tension & pressure, the temperature goes up.

I check out everyone on my walkie-talkie; I'm the only guy allowed to talk.

— 2.08. Read me? Over.

The accomplice waiting in the truck at the traffic circle, who will alert the rest of us when the Brinks passes by, replies: — Copy. Nothing yet.

— 2.09. Are you in place? Over.

— Affirmative.

So as not to be noticed, the guy's not behind the wheel but waiting in the back. He'll have to get into the driver's side to start the truck.

I look to Bruno.

— You all right?

— Yeah, we'll be ok.

— Don't worry. Everything's going to go super smooth.

I've got to keep up their spirits. Just like a soccer team before a match.

— Don't worry, guys. Feel at home. We've got an open road.

Courage is contagious. The guys are overwhelmed with doubt but have to be thinking, — Listen to him! This guy is something else.

Everybody's focused. Two minutes later:

— 2.08. Read me?

— Roger.

— *The train is entering the station.*

That's it! We shoot out the door like bullets. The street is deserted. I get behind the wheel of the Safrane. I pass in front of the Peugeot Expert. The others climb into the Audi and the cars all follow me in single file.

— 2.08. Read me?

— How goes it?

— We're at the traffic circle.

I play with the accelerator, hot to plow into the Brinks and smash the wheelbase. To storm out and take them. Now we're into it — completely. Fear's got no place. Let's go!

— *Is it there, or no?*

— *No—wait. There it is! Here it comes.*

I count to nine. I start moving and see the Brinks. It comes onto the road moving slowly. I move toward it in the opposite direction and, just as it approaches, I plow into the left front wheel. A huge blast. The air bag doesn't deploy. The driver thinks it's an accident. I get out of the car. At six feet tall, I'm pretty imposing. I brandish the M16...

— *Get out! Now! Out!*

The guy stares at me while the Peugeot Expert stops in front. So far, so good. Except for the van, driven by one of our two new recruits, was supposed to stop at the end of the roadway and block police access. Instead, it moves toward us and stops just behind the Brinks.

I keep screaming: *"Out! Out! Get out of the truck!"*

The guy turns his head to see the beur bursting out of the Peugeot Expert and thrusting an MG-42 between the windshield and the open door on the driver's side. And now Bruno and Stéphane appear with their Kalashnikovs. In five seconds all four of us are face-to-face with the truck.

— *Open! Get out! We're going to blow you up!*

I drop the M16 & sling it over my shoulder. I open the backpack and take out the plastic explosive. Now the chief guard, an old grey-haired guy, stands up and says calmly:

— We're getting out.

Amazing. Under 45 seconds, they're opening the door.

— *Your weapons!*

I bring out the first one, then the second. I cuff their hands behind their backs using Serflex. I take their .357 Magnums & toss them over the fence by the road. Only the chief stays inside, to open the safe. My partner gets ready to take the cash. Now the chief says:

— I can't open the safe with the side door open. They work together.

— Don't try to be a hero, I say calmly but firmly. Think of your wife and children. We don't have time.

— Okay, sir.

I shut the side door and turn to him: We'll do it at the count of three... 1, 2, and 3!

But I go too fast for him and it doesn't work.

— Are you fucking with me?

— No, I'm not.

— Okay. Let's try again: 1, 2, 3!

This time, it opens. He doesn't get time to move an inch before I grab him by the shoulder and shove him out of the truck. He tumbles to the ground and I cuff him.

— Don't be an idiot!

Coming out, I'd glanced inside the truck and saw right away there were way too many bags. *Shit.*

It sucks not to be able to take it all! We'll be getting away with only 2,000,000,000 to 3,000,000,000 francs instead of 10,000,000,000. I blame myself. It counts as a serious mistake not to have foreseen this.

Meanwhile now comes a car. My M16 in hand, I signal the driver to stop. He doesn't stop, though, but makes a U-turn. After that, from the other direction, a big truck. I move toward it, brandishing the M16.

— *Come down! Get out of the truck!*

The driver steps out. I slam the door shut and tell the guy to get lost.

He took off like a bullet.

Hoping to seize as many bags as possible, we've got to bring the cars closer. I take the wheel of the first Audi and put down the M16, which hampers my movements. Put it in gear, first forward, then reverse. Once in position, I open the doors and trunk, leave the engine running, and go on to the second car. Suddenly it hits me: *this is too easy*. What's happening is unbelievable. Wheel broken, the guys opened the door in two seconds. Inside billions are waiting. Are you a genius or what? *It's too simple.*

With the second car, it takes a single U-turn. Then into reverse:

— *Let's go, guys! Hurry up! The sacks! Grab the sacks!*

We've lost one minute opening the armored truck and getting into the vault. We're already three minutes, 30 seconds. What's happening? The guys are bringing out the bags but not yet filling up the trunk. That's because the fucking guards had piled bags full of coins on top of the sacks of cash. We have to get rid of the ones on top before reaching the good stuff. It's a mess!

Suddenly we hear *ping-bong, ping-bong*.

The cops are arriving faster than we thought. Instead of 4 minutes 15 seconds, they're here at 3 minutes 45 seconds. That's because the truck that was supposed to be positioned to slow the police wasn't there.

The beur shouts: — *Police! They're here!*

He's armed with grenades and a .38 special. But he backs up toward his car. He's about to flee. He's scared. And now I see the BAC's gray Peugeot 306. Those cops had guessed at first that the depot was under attack and the armored truck was just stopped in some kind of traffic jam. But when they see me wearing a hockey mask and standing in the middle of the road, they understand. One of them comes out, his bulletproof vest hanging off him. He didn't have time to fasten it. While I take the .357 out of the backpack — I left my M16 in the car — he shoots. I take a bullet in my shoulder. I go down.

Not even two seconds later, I hear a flurry of bullets. Behind me, Bruno is unloading his Kalashnikov on the little Peugeot. Four cops dive out of the car and hit the pavement. They're flat on the ground among pines trees and lie motionless, hands protecting their heads. They don't move. I hear Bruno, still shooting, shout:

— *Cocksucker motherfuckers!*

And Stéphane, screaming:

— *Go on, take them out!*

By reflex, I get up.

— *Goddammit! I'm hit.*

The pain was so bad, I had the feeling my arm must actually be lying on the ground. I feel for it with my right hand and realize it's still attached.

I jump into the Audi but can't take the wheel. I change positions with Stéphane. The car trunks are full but we leave behind billions! We take the first right turn and check back to see we didn't leave anybody behind. We'll find out later that, thanks to the barrage from the assault rifle, nobody risked pursuing us. We could have driven away going twenty miles an hour.

The BAC put out an all-points bulletin. But nobody comes after us.

At Roissy, we change cars as planned. We load the bags and speed along the A1 toward Oise. The day before we'd sawed through a maintenance fence along the highway to avoid the toll booth. Driving on side roads, we reach the hideout. To avoid ever being welcomed by the BRI,* you never go back where you started. That's the golden rule. Despite living apart & anonymously, and exercising extreme discretion when planning armed robberies, you could be traced. And most of the time, they'd be waiting for you. Before the attack, they're not interested, because you're

---

* Brigade de Recherche et d'Intervention, an anti-gang police force that targets serious crimes such as armed robbery with kidnapping and hostage-taking.

not worth that much. And at the moment of the attack, they see it as too risky.

Once we're at the hideout — an apartment in a residential building — we need to call a doctor. Because of the bleeding, I can't go out. I'm not suffering much but I'm white as a sheet. My buddies' eyes glisten; they're on the verge of tears. They'd take my place if they could. There's dead silence.

I tell Bruno to load the gun that's still in my backpack.

— Why? What are you going to do?

— *Load the gun!*

He loads it. I tell them:

— If anybody wants to take me to the hospital, I'll kill him. Do what you've got to do to find me a doctor.

I won't go into the details, but we found somebody who came three hours later. Stéphane found him and went to get him. He opens me up.

— You're lucky, sir!

The bullet had passed through the muscle that connects the arm and the shoulder blade. It exited through the armpit, harming neither bones nor internal organs.

— From now on you've got to play the lotto.

The doctor uses an entire bottle of Betadine, gives me an injection & some pills. Then he fixes a splint and makes an appointment for an X-ray at a clinic two days later.

I stay alone in the apartment. Have I just cheated death, or do we call it a miracle? Probably cheated, because if the bullet hadn't come out through my armpit, I'd be dead. I see the doctor once more. At the Hotel Concorde Lafayette, where I book a suite, he brings his medical bag & a large sterilized sheet. After local anesthesia, he treats me. He puts on a new splint. I'm able to drive. Two weeks later I take off the splint, it's started to heal.

I go back to the doctor and offer him 200,000 francs, which he refuses.

Meanwhile, the others have gone on vacation. We'll meet again in September for a debrief. We have plenty of questions. Should we keep on doing Brinks trucks? Considering the danger, is it worth it? Should we risk bringing in others? With the two new guys, it didn't work. We now realize that this world of grand larceny is filled with big mouths and show-offs. We've got to be very careful. It's a world of jealousy and guys who aren't all that good on the ground. So we decide to break with the whole lot of them.

Stéphane & Bruno are still really pissed off. With both, but especially with the guy who didn't place the truck where he was supposed to at Villepinte.

— I'm not working with them again.

— They're nothing but shits from the *banlieue*.

That's not the story I've heard. Three days *before* Villepinte, there was another attack on an armored truck in Paris that was carried out using a dump truck, just like in *Heat*.

It's true. And what about it?

According to what I've been told, it was you. Should I tell you about it?

I love good stories!

Your Israelian friend was unavailable, so you brought in a 20-year-old with whom you'd done a lot of petty thievery when you were young. As a driver, he was out of this world. He agreed right away to the dump truck. But he's never done it before so he called on a friend who'd been a truck driver for 20 years. This guy arrived with a big rig and showed him how. The guy was so terrific it took him just an hour to learn how to drive, parallel park bumper-to-bumper, and go in reverse. As a result, he went out and stole a front-loading dump truck, which he parked at the company where your father worked. You went with him to change the license plates, dressed in work clothes and a hard hat.

Then you performed practice simulations in the woods. On the ground, you drew the outline of an armored truck. In front of it, a three-man commando unit positioned a rocket launcher that your driver had brought back from Belgium, where he often went to buy stolen car registrations. The same mechanic supplied the rocket launcher and would later provide you with the Kalashnikovs.

During the simulations, you weren't aiming the rocket launchers at the Brinks because the guards weren't stupid. They know that to fire one, you've got to be a football field away. You only want to prove that you're seriously tough. You want to force them to open the door by threatening to tear open the windshield with explosives — but that's more bluff. You know you'd risk killing the guards. One of you got another idea from watching TV. During a fire at the basilica in Florence, a fireman broke open a bulletproof vitrine protecting a precious relic that absolutely had to be saved. He simply used a sledgehammer. So you bought one in a hardware store — in case the guards wouldn't open up.

You went on to use the simulations to answer various questions. Who would take the guards out of the truck? Who will keep them covered? Who will grab the sacks of money? Who'll drive the car? You'll need to adjust the rear-view mirrors, etc. Who will be in the front seat, who the back? Where do you change cars? You'll decide on Fresnes, which is a sort of wink and nod to your brother, who's in prison there. But it's also near Orly, where you'll leave the relay cars. You learned from *Heat* that helicopters aren't allowed to fly over airports.

You also planned to use a car to slow down the Brinks before the collision with the dump truck. And still another car to follow it in order to keep other vehicles away during the heist itself.

Your found your hideout after the robbery thanks to an acquaintance who took a vacation that you paid for. The relay cars at Orly would remain in long-term parking at 50 francs a day. You'll be six altogether on the job: you, Bruno, Stéphane, the driver of the dump truck, and the two guys who'll be with you a month later for the job in Villepinte. Those two you'll keep at arm's length. During the attack, they'll be positioned to stop oncoming traffic. They're guests on this job and you don't want to assign them anything more dangerous.

Once the Brinks moves past the junction and gets onto the highway, the beur will set out detour signs and direct traffic.

Do you want me to go on?

Sure, go ahead...

Police attribute this attack to you because, like at Villepinte — & in the movie *Heat* —, the perpetrators wore hockey masks.

As with the first robbery, you didn't fire on the Brinks, nor did you hurt or insult the guards, and newspapers the next day commended your performance: *"If armed robbery was an honorable profession, workers like these would be some of the best in France."* They saw you as consummate professionals. You've said yourself that you thought the masks would be a fine signature — that on future jobs, guards will recognize you and open the doors.

After the success of Villepinte, it seems you had imitators who operated the same way.

Which took us by complete surprise. It got to be a fashion. By September we were outdone by others. There were several gangs that flourished in and around Paris. In October, two or three attacks on armored trucks, then seven or eight in December. Explosives were used in the attack on the ACDS depot in Vert-le-Grand. Attacks on armored trucks were carried out at Orly, Rungis, Aulnay-sous-Bois, Porte de la Chapelle. Totally crazy. Then in January, two or three attacks; in February, even more.

The year 1997 would set a record for attacks in Paris. We inspired guys from the projects. They've read the newspapers. "Fuck, they did it like *Heat*, with assault weapons." It gave them courage and created a craze. Everybody climbed aboard.

The two guys we let go set up their own little group in their project in the 93rd. In November 1997, they attacked an ACDS truck in the 11th arrondissement near Place de la Nation. They carried it out with Antonio Lagès a.k.a. "The Portuguese."* They managed to drag out two of the three guards but the third one locked himself in the truck and succeeded in driving off.

Lots of fiascos. After ours, of seven attacks on armored trucks in Paris, only two succeeded.

And what about you?

Something completely crazy happened. At the end of November, we decided to case a depot in Vert-le-Grand.† Three or four buildings that belonged to ACDS were located in an industrial park there. We planned an attack on one of its big armored trucks, which returned to the depot every Thursday evening with a good part of the weekly haul from supermarkets, and also cash from the Banque de France that would refill the ATMs at the end of the week. Sometimes it came back at 8:00 PM, other times at 10:00 PM. When the truck signaled its arrival, they would open the depot and three or four armed guards

* Assassinated gangland style in 2000.
† A city in the department of Essonne, near Paris.

would come out to wait for it. It was a big delivery. They were on high alert.

So early evening every Thursday, we'd arrive in a surveillance van as it got dark. I'd already dropped off an accomplice around 5:00 PM. He'd hide behind a hedge of bushes just in front of the depot, and stay there until I returned about 7:00 or 8:00 PM. If he needed to, he'd piss into a plastic bottle to avoid leaving DNA. He had a Kenwood walkie-talkie in order to communicate with me while I'm watching what comes and goes around the traffic circle.

We position another lookout in front of the depot, hidden in a thicket of trees near a garage. One night, during the stakeout, a little van arrives. It slows down and drops off a guy who hides in the same place.

It sounds crazy but we're two gangs casing the same joint.

The other gang was not so careful. My accomplice would pretend to be hitchhiking when I dropped him off, and then walk until he reached the thickets. The other guys seem professional enough, but overconfident. Their driver stops right in front. The guy who gets out is huge and he's dressed all in black. My accomplice crouches a little distance away but goes unnoticed and doesn't move. As soon as the other guy gets settled, he's on his walkie-talkie, saying: "Ok, I'm in position."

Hoping that I might understand what was going on, my accomplice only presses the button of his walkie-talkie. He doesn't say a word. I hear cars passing & wonder what he's doing. When the time comes,

I go to pick him up. I drive by, but nobody's there. I call him on the walkie-talkie:

— What's going on? I'm here!

Dead air. I take off, then make a second pass.

— Damn it — are you there?

I punch the horn. The guy from the other gang must have been wondering if it wasn't meant for him.

A fucking mess.

I go to pick up the other guy, and together we go back to see. He gets out, goes in among the trees, and comes out with our buddy.

— You'll never guess. There's another guy on lookout. We're in the same game.

— Stop joking...

He gives me the lowdown but now, in addition, he's forgotten his plastic bottle. He goes to get it & by the time he comes back, another van has arrived for the other guy. We check each other out and make a little gesture that signals we know what's up. We never saw them again.

Much later, in prison, I tell this story to a big member of the Dream Team. He smiles and tells me he knows the story already. His buddy was the guy in the thicket.

Anyway, on Saturday, December 17, 1997, a front-loading dump truck, stolen from around Porte de Versailles, would attack the depot. Thieves would use the truck to break through the security entrance. Michel Crutel, who was still with the gang, was the first inside. They then used explosives to blow open the armored doors and grab the cash in the counting room: 18,000,000 francs, or a little less than 3,000,000 euros.

Had you given up on the idea?

No. We waited for the depot to reopen after that attack. It was closed while under reconstruction. To learn more, we started hanging out in a nearby bistro. We talked with the owner, who was a soccer fan. We let him think we were from Corbeil and wanted to join the village soccer club. The local field seemed nice and we'd like to start practicing as soon as we could. The guy told us the players were pretty good and occasionally stopped by for a drink. At that point I turned to Stéphane:

— And you know, this isn't just any old place. This is where they had all those attacks.

The owner's eyes got big. Here was a chance for him to shine and tell his stories.

— What attacks? asked Stéphane.

— The armored truck robberies

— That didn't happen here?

The owner cut in: You bet it did.

He told us how the depot had been previously attacked, back in 1995.

— That was quite something. They took everybody hostage.

It was true. Michael Crutel and his partners, in 1995, had already got away with 35,000,000 francs. The Hornec brothers* were suspects at the time, but it wasn't them.

---

* A well-known *&* powerful gang from Montreuil.

The owner "informed" us that the depot was closed for now.

— It had to be. Thieves blew the place wide open. They planted explosives on the hinges.

The guards were regular customers and they told him everything.

Especially about that attack six months earlier.

— The guys certainly didn't rack their brains figuring it. They brought in a dump truck & carried out the attack just like in *Heat*. Have you seen the movie? They did the same thing right here on the highway.

— Is that right?

— They cut off traffic in both directions and sent the truck barreling into the armored vehicle. Nobody killed or hurt… The cops who come here for lunch told me that it was grand larceny — super well done…

— Sure. So when are they going to reopen the depot?

— Well, I've heard that they're not going to reopen.

He was right. A month later, ACDS went bankrupt.

So we found ourselves like kids from the projects with fuck-all and bored. — *We're begging you, Please! Re-open!*

Meanwhile, again according to my sources, you're going to carry out a third job before going onto a new one. But this time it'll be a failure.

This was to go down at Seine-et-Marne, where you were going to steal supermarket cash deposits. You'd checked out the business, observed the comings and goings of the armored trucks, and opted for Carrefour, the big grocery store in Meaux. The usual haul to the depot was 1,000,000–2,000,000 francs. You've let your two newcomers go but retained the pyrotechnician. So you're five altogether, including you, Bruno, Stéphane, and the driver. One of you is going to take care of immobilizing the truck and also bringing up the getaway cars. Another will take care of the guards. A third will grab the good sacks but leave the coins, credit cards, & checks. The fourth guy is to be in charge of loading them in the cars. And a fifth guy covers the other four. To block the armored vehicle, you plan on stopping it *à la Marseillaise* — that is, sandwiching it between two trucks, one behind and the other in front. You weren't entirely in favor of that, but it's the technique the driver wants to use.

As the job commences, the truck crashes into the front of the vehicle, but the guard who's driving manages to keep moving even though he's thoroughly stunned by the shock. No shots were fired.

At this point, one of you zooms up in a getaway car, sizes up the scene, but can't let it go. "*Fuck.* We just wasted three months and knocked ourselves out for nothing. All because last time that other gang blasted the depot to kingdom come. And now this guy thinks he's going to escape? No way." And so now *he* plows into the armored truck. But the driver, still in shock, punches into reverse and manages to get back to the depot. Where he's praised as a hero!

Things on your side are tense. The guy having crashed the getaway car into the Brinks, now you've got to flee the scene on foot. But you've got to set fire to the car, which will keep you close by just as people start coming out to look.

You stick around to do that and as you join the others you retrieve the rocket-launcher and assault rifle. As the panic subsides, you're back in control and immediately target a couple driving a nice big Renault. It was like this:

— Get out of the car. Immediately.

— Just wait one moment, sir, and I'll park it.

— *Get out of the fucking car! Now!*

— Come on, Bernard! Get out of the car! Leave it!

— Okay, guys. Jump in!

The driver takes the wheel, you beside him, the three others in the back. Now a siren blares. It's the village firemen. People come out with shotguns and somebody flings a soda can at the car. It's the Resistance!

You manage to get out of the village, but the driver goes too fast. The car careens onto the sidewalk and a tire blows out. As another car arrives, you plant yourselves in the middle of the road, some of you armed with rocket launchers, others with Kalashnikovs. You scream:

— *Stop! Stop!*

The guy gives up his car and a service road takes you back onto the highway. The driver continues to speed like a madman, zigzagging through traffic. Even though it doesn't matter, now you've changed cars.

Flashing gumballs appear once you reach the Francilienne. The only sound inside the car is that of guns reloading. But everybody's calm and nobody's going to fire because, just after passing Villepinte, you've got traffic jams. And the driver, swerving between cars & barely missing them, managed to get past the congestion faster than the police.

So you leave the highway just ahead of Roissy and change cars at the airport parking lot. Everybody makes fun of the driver.

— Ah! Beautiful technique, the Marseillaise! Truck in front, truck in back. You total fuckup... From now on, be stupid on your own.

And you take off for a month.

I'll be damned if people don't tell you some nice stories.

So what do you do now?

I leave for Israel. To do that I've got a technique, using forged papers. To begin, I take the TGV first class to Geneva. In suit and tie, a garment bag over my shoulder. At customs they don't even look at me and barely glance at my passport. So much for profiling!

Arriving that evening at the Mövenpick Hotel, I leave my ticket at the desk to insure trust. Then, a little trick. I take the early morning flight from Geneva to Zurich, arriving at 8:00 A M. At the gate in Geneva, the Swiss Air hostess gives me a second boarding pass and I ask them to forward my luggage to Tel Aviv. I buy newspapers, my Armani coat on my arm, and mingle with the bankers leaving for Zurich. Nobody asks for ID. We're not yet post-September 11. At Zurich, there's no need even to change terminals. I board the plane for Tel Aviv without being checked. When I land, the customs officer sees I've come from Paris and passed through both Geneva and Zurich. He's not in the least suspicious even though nobody's actually checked my passport.

At customs, rather than try to blend in with the crowd, I'm first in line. An old soul taught me that. You'd have to be dead to be more up front. You must not overact, pretend to be a man in a hurry. I relax, unbutton my shirt, act like I just woke up and look the officer straight in the eye. Then, when Israeli security asks why I'm here, I tell the truth. I've got friends in Israel. That's all. Then it's: "Goodbye. Enjoy your visit."

What are you planning to do in Tel Aviv?

Eat & sleep, get back on my feet.

In France, I'm anxious. I can't stop throwing up and using the toilet. To relieve the pressure, some people use drugs or alcohol, or go to prostitutes. In my case, I become almost anorexic. I eat and a minute later throw up. It's part of the stress and tension, concentration and physical conditioning.

We stayed in Tel Aviv. Daily life was simple. At the time I had a girlfriend who was a student at the university and I live nearby in an upscale neighborhood. My friends live in Herzliya, a sort of Neuilly-sur-Seine, but on the ocean.

Mornings I wake up early and drive my girlfriend to school at 8:00 A M. She takes intensive lessons to learn Hebrew.

What do you do for money?

I've got an arrangement with some feuj. One of my friends knows a guy who works in a currency exchange in Paris. I went to meet him and he assured me that a transfer to a bank account would take 24 hours and the money would be available a day later. In cash. He took 3 per cent. I trusted him. Two days later, somebody in Israel went to the bank and withdrew the cash.

It's not hard to open an account in an Israeli bank. They just asked for identification. I deposited $30,000 and with shekels opened a second account. The woman was shocked to see that I was walking around with that kind of money. She warned me to watch out for thieves.

To find an apartment in Ramat-Aviv, I went through a real estate agency. The person I dealt with spoke French.

— I'm a newly-arrived immigrant. I've come to do my *aliya* and am thinking of buying some property. But in the meantime, I'm looking for a rental.

She likes the way I talk. I explain that I've left Paris because it was too difficult to stay kosher. I talk about Ben Gurion — I was pretty good in history at school — about the State of Israel, about my love for Yitzhak Rabin. Simply put, I smooth talk her and soon she loves me like a son. All the more knowing I'm rolling in dough!

— Where do you want to live?
— Someplace new.

She finds me a beautiful apartment with marble floors, three bedrooms and the same number of bathrooms, a jacuzzi, fully equipped kitchen, and a big terrace.

— Exactly what I want.

— It rents for $1,400. Do you have pay stubs?

— No, I'm a new immigrant.

— Ouch. The owner's going to want a guarantor.

— If you want, I'll pay him every six months in advance.

— You can do that?

— I can even do it in cash, if you want.

The owner wants to meet with me. He's a lawyer, very nice guy. The woman makes a deal with him, lowering my rent to 800. The notary likes me and offers financial help when I move in. I've told them that I'd like to open a restaurant. And as for the woman, she's inviting me to family get-togethers. She tells me not to buy anything for now, she has a brother who manages a shopping mall and can get me reduced prices. So soon I'm all settled. I still have to buy a car. At the BMW dealer, I pay cash. The guy gives me a kiss when I leave.

All nice people but I need to keep my distance.

I pass my time in and around Tayelet Promenade, on the waterfront in Tel Aviv. My days are spent at the Dan Hotel, where I'm a member of the club there. It's a superb place to meet friends.

And where you also have an unexpected encounter.

Leaving the Dan with Bruno, we run smack into Ehud Barak, who's just taken over the Labor Party after Shimon Peres lost the election to Netanyahu. We shake his hand and tell him how much we like him.

Bruno runs into a nearby store and makes him the gift of a watch.

I quickly learn Hebrew, taking courses at the Ulpan. There I meet plenty of French people. From now on I feel at home.

On weekends I go to Eilat, stay at the Holiday Inn and visit the great historical sites. At Ein Gedi, I free-climb a beautiful mountain with two friends. We're dying from the heat. But reaching the peak, we can see Jordan on the other side. My friends are exhausted.

— Look! The Promised Land!

And there, my friend, palm trees, an oasis, orchards, a waterfall. *Magnificent.* We swim in the crystal-clear water. A stunning place. It was like this in the Garden of Eden...

Masada, on the other hand, tells me something much different. Battling the Romans, Jews preferred death to surrender. It's where a lot of people celebrate bar mitzvah. Also here the soldiers of Tsahal take their oath. But more, the history of it can't help but come to mind. The view of the Negev is grand. I fall in love with the desert. It makes me think that in my country, Algeria, there's the Sahara. But I've never seen it.

I also visit the Arab section of Jerusalem, the "Green Line" with the Palestinians. I tell them I'm Algerian. They think that I'm a Sephardic Jew and don't trust me. When I meet an auto mechanic from Algeria, he can tell by my accent.

— What are you doing here?

— Hey, I'm on vacation.

He doesn't understand why I would vacation in a place like this. He's married to a Palestinian.

Life in Israel is pleasant but as soon as you leave East Jerusalem you can see the deprivation in which the Palestinian people live. I don't fill up with anger and rage because it's not part of my nature. But I tell myself it's truly unjust. Sometimes in Israel I'd hear Arabs insulted, a fact that makes me think of how much I value my friends. One day, in a taxi with Stéphane, the driver tells us that he never goes to France because of all the Arabs. Obviously, I don't react. But Stéphane takes my hand as a mother would her child. The driver could sense he'd said something stupid.

I was touched too when I saw a Rabbi in discussion with an Imam, as if Israeli and Arabs could manage to get along. I've got to say that this all happened in 1997, when things were not so bad.

I adjust to living in Israel and I'm comfortable. But there's a problem. I'm bored. My partners and I are addicted to the adrenaline rush. We don't know what to do with ourselves.

You could have enjoyed life.

We don't know how. Our shitty life is what we're used to. We miss armed robbery. Just like people get hungry and eat, we need to rob at gunpoint.

We took the wrong path. The problem is that it's not a path or even a road but a superhighway. We drove at full speed. And on a superhighway there's no traffic circle to send you back the other way. You can't stop. You must drive to the next toll booth or the next exit. And for us the off-ramp has two names: prison or death.

Business goes well. One job after another, every three months. We don't make billions, but we're happy... We organize our lives between Tel Aviv and France.

And, like anybody who's anybody, we go to Spain and visit Costa Del Sol.

What takes you there?

At first we just went on vacation. Then we read that it's a good place to hide out. So we checked out prices for a place to rent. We learned you didn't need identification, same thing for a car. In short, an easy way to put another degree of separation between us and France.

As soon as we got to Marbella, we ran into my buddy, the drug dealer & fence from the 93rd, who'd furnished us with guns. We were parked in front of Zara's, the department store. Our car was a Clio Baccara, plate number 60. He recognized us and suggested meeting that evening at the Olivia Valere, a discotheque. People were standing in line outside but thanks to our friend, we were brought in through the back door. Our friend was well-respected and whenever we went back without him, the owner always welcomed us with a big smile.

Once seated at one of the best of the VIP tables, we were surrounded by famous people like Sean

Connery, Mick Hucknall (singer with the band Simply Red), Linda Evangelista, Naomi Campbell. But also some call girls. A buddy I knew from Creil went for Adrian Paul's sister-in-law, an Italian woman; he dated her, in fact, and we were later invited to a party in Paul's villa. I didn't feel like going; I preferred looking for movies to watch on VHS — good French films starring Belmondo, Gabin, Ventura... the world of gangsters. We were renting a beautiful Moroccan-style villa with a huge TV screen in the living room. But my buddies went to Adrian Paul's party, then they were invited by Prince's girlfriend to her place, and after that to Sean Connery's.

Occasionally, I'd go clubbing with them. One night my friend and I were about to sit down for a drink when he said: Look at the guy at the next table.

It was Francis the Belge. We recognized him from the newspapers. *Francis the Belge!* That could only mean the place was seriously hot and dangerous. It was brimming with the underworld. So right then we decided to move to the bar. The Belge kept turning around like he was paranoid about something. He was with two or three guys — legends of the Lyon and Marseilles underworld. As we were leaving the table to walk to the bar, we noticed that one of his men also got up, and he and another guy took seats not far from us. They were in paranoid mode. Just looking at us, they knew that we were French and wonder who sent us. Then the nightclub owner comes over to greet us. Right away the Belge follows, and we're introduced...

— Francis, meet these guys, they're super.

The Belge seems reassured. He invites us to have a drink with him.

I never went back to the clubs in Marbella.* The local nightlife included a lot of big shots from the southern banlieues. They went there looking for new recruits. With the idea of bringing them aboard as dealers. There was one who was looking to get the skinny on us. *Who are these guys? Where do they live?* When he got wise that we were with the boss, he let it drop. Our friend called those big shots "The Apaches" because they acted like they were perched atop the mountain, watching people arrive, ready to come down and fuck them up. If they caught you, they could make you suffer. They could chop you to pieces. They were brutal.

Other guys from the suburbs were there?

Yeah, quite a few from Seine-Saint-Denis, Val-de-Marne, & Essonne... And a good many from Lyon & Marseilles.

Actually, I became friends with a beur from just north of Marseilles. A guy who'd followed the same path as me but in the drug business. I'd go to La Canebière† just to meet and party with him.

---

* The popular resort city, also known for celebrity villas and wealthy clientele, is indeed considered an international haven for organized criminals involved in illicit drugs, & hence, violence and reprisals.

† A famed street in Marseilles.

Did you yourself avoid getting involved with them, or was it the supposed antagonism between Parisians & the Marseillais that kept you from working with them?

Not at all! We had nothing in common in terms of activities and so no opportunity. Those clichés die hard, this stupidity that pits Paris against Marseilles. According to the way young thugs from Marseilles think, there are no Parisians, blacks, beurs, or Chinese. Only the brave on one hand and fucking idiots on the other. Which is why I like them.

Same thing for the Lyonnais. In addition to older guys from Vaulx-en-Velin who are highly respected, there are plenty of good guys in the projects in Lyon. I've crossed their paths often; liked and appreciated them.

Let's go back to Costa del Sol. The guys there were all into drugs?

All of them were into chocolate, the shit (hashish). Most bought from the same guy. But in Costal del Sol itself you smell powder — gunpowder. There's a lot of tension and settling of scores. Even the Spanish police, when they stop you on patrol, get panicky when they realize you're French.

We stayed three months in Marbella. A snake pit and at the same time the eagle's nest. It's a snake pit because you had these big gangs that, instead of meeting in the slammer, they get together in Marbella. It's kind of like the floor of the stock exchange, except it's armed robbery...

— Want hashish? Easy...

— Coke? No problem...

— Planning a hit? What about guns? No problem...

— You want cars? No problem...

Worse, here's where you can develop contacts in Paris, Lyon, & Marseilles. Better than a prison yard and what's more, you're on the outside. Here too is where young guys can meet ones who are older and more experienced. Like nowhere else. All the help you need can be found right here. Of course, the Belge or somebody like him, if he doesn't know you, won't work with you even if you're introduced. Older guys are afraid of the young rebeurs, but some of them have been around for so long that they get together anyway.

But Costa Del Sol wasn't for us. Our circle of friends was smaller than in Paris. Also, with all these thugs, the place was full of cops.

Soon after I was back in France, I left for New York to be with a girlfriend who lived there. I thought of moving there. I love the city, the people are warm & friendly. And as I had enough money, everything was good. But I missed Tel Aviv.

Except in 1998, when you found yourself a little on the lonely side.

A fair number of my friends went to prison that year. Stéphane was caught for some stupid thing in Israel. Cops checked his papers and realized they were fake. So they searched his place & found a gun.

He took a bullet — a year in jail. Bruno, he went away, too. Drug trafficking. He'd gone into it with a guy who ratted him out. He got three years. Another guy who worked with us got caught for auto theft. In a parking lot, undercovers of the Senlis gendarmerie were on the lookout in an unmarked car and they arrested him. He had half a dozen boosted, repainted cars parked there. And he was already wanted for armed robbery after a snitch gave him up.

The cops didn't make any connection to me. But paranoia made us think they were onto us & just pretending not to know. Paranoia is a big thing among armed robbers. I had to get out of there.

Not even counting the fact I was already known to be involved in bank robberies and jewelry heists in Oise, not to mention RAM, my blood was all over the scene in Villepinte. So the day I was arrested would be the day they knew who I was... It got to be too much.

If I'd run into somebody older than me, he would have advised me to go straight for a few years and let things cool off.

But I didn't do that. I decided to return to France. I had plenty of projects in the works. A problem, though, was I lacked partners... In Creil, a buddy who was dealing drugs suggested a new partner:

— If you need help dealing with armored transportation, I know somebody. He's up for it, a little nuts, but very good.

— Let's meet him!

It didn't start well. The guy picked the Champs-Élysées as a meeting spot. What the fuck's that about?

Champs-Élysées! Not exactly the most discreet place in the world. It's under constant major surveillance. Kids from the projects all hang out there. The 8th arrondissement is their territory... The guys roam the likes of rue Ponthieu, François 1er... All the bars and nightspots and strip clubs that crisscross and run perpendicular to Champs-Élysées are teeming with thieves and outlaws. So too, of course, cops...

Moreover, the guy wanted to meet at 11:00 at night. We're going to be with the regular customers of the 36th* who wake up at 3:00 in the afternoon. Those guys aren't morning people...

I went anyway. As soon as I walked into the brasserie, I spotted him: shaved head, khaki tracksuit, not turning his back to the front window... I'd later learn that he was in plenty of trouble in Paris: he'd shot guys and been shot himself...

Here he's by himself, but there's a marmoset wrapped around his shoulders and climbing upside his head... All the chicks from the bar wanted to play with it.

What to make of this character!? I'd been told he was okay. Even if he'd never taken part in an armored truck hit, he was one serious hardcore guy. And he wanted to make a lot of money. He introduced himself:

— Nordine. But everybody calls me Nono.

He was also nicknamed *Le Barge* or *Le Dingue* — Crazy Man or Nutcase. He was a year or two older than me. A perfect specimen of a criminal from the

---

* Police Headquarters in Paris.

projects. We talked a while and I let him know I needed guns. He had them.

— I have one of each: a Kalashnikov, an M16, and an AR/M16. Ammo and bulletproof vests...

The guy was interesting. I didn't think he was fronting but I had to make sure. We made an appointment to meet in a few days, and he'd show me his arsenal. The guns were real but he couldn't fit the magazines in the rifles. That was no big deal because my Israeli buddy, the arms specialist, was just then in Paris. He came to see us, took apart and reassembled the rifles in front of us. This time, the cartridges fit perfectly. Nono was astounded. It turned out he'd been trying to make the assault rifles work for six months without success. And in two minutes my buddy solved the problem.

So Nono seemed fearless and had the gear we needed. I told him about my plans to take down an armored vehicle.

— I've got another friend who might be interested.
— Really?

We talked a while about armed robbery in general. He told me about his gangs. He quickly made me to understand that he was close to the circle around Jean-Pierre Lepape.*

---

* A criminal from the southern banlieue, Jean-Pierre Lepape was assassinated in a bar in Vitry-sur-Seine in 1998 by two men armed with shotguns. A gangster with a record, he was known for a gun battle with police in 1977. Never found guilty for his armed robberies, he turned to drug dealing in the mid-1980s. [Note by J. Pierrat.]

Had you ever heard of this Nono before?

I'd heard and read about big names in armed robbery from newspapers and books. But when it came
to tough customers from the projects, even guys like
me didn't know about them. But I sensed right away
that here was somebody involved with big-name
criminals around Paris.

Nono could come up with guns, stolen cars, fake
IDs, and he also had good contacts in the drug business. He had three or four portable phones that he
used for business. Above all, he made me realize that
he had a certain allure for the new generation coming out of Paris and Hauts-de-Seine. They respected
but also feared him.

This was a very dangerous guy. When I met him
the first time for a drink at the brasserie, there was
a pen on the table... I started to fiddle with it. Suddenly Nono:

— *Hey-hey-hey!* Don't touch that pen!
— Okay — why not?
— Why? It's loaded: it's got two .22 longs inside...

If anybody came aiming to waste him, he was
ready with his pistol-pen. This guy was *equipped*.

At our third meeting, Nono started to dig and ap-
preciate me, which was wild... He also tested me. So
he quickly understood who I was. Until then he'd
only read about my stuff in the papers. Now he found
out who I really was.

At that moment, I began to realize it, too. I was
"known" in the projects. Indirectly, by what I'd done.

Guys stated to talk about me. I'd always opted for discretion, for silence. But my acts had got ahead of me.

Nono started taking me to his favorite hangouts. A day spent with Nono was a crazy fucking day... I got into the projects, prowling among the beasts of the jungle.

One morning, we had to go test the guns. I gave him an early appointment. He wasn't usually up early, but he came. On the way he wanted to pick up money from a few of his guys. Okay by me. I went with him. I thought I knew Paris and had covered about every inch of it. But Nono showed me I'd seen nothing yet. We went into projects where I'd never set foot in the 20th, 19th, 15th. He passed quickly along the ground floor, and guys slipped him envelopes. He didn't get billions, but 30,000 francs here, 60,000 there. He talked just a little with the guys:

— *How've you been?*
— *Eh, not bad... How's the family?*
— *Great. Okay, no time. So long!*

This money was coming from where?

Drugs. Cocaine *&* hash. He brought them back from Spain with an associate. Later I learned that the hashish was not all his; he was the wholesaler. Because he was known as a killer, a nutcase and overall dangerous character, he was in charge of collecting the money. Eventually I'd learn that his bosses were some of the biggest names among old-style hoodlums in the eastern and southern banlieues, and also a few serious traffickers from the projects in Hauts-de-Seine. In short, Nono had a rep.

One day, in the Lafayette-Concorde Hotel with Nono and his associate, we ran into Marc, the youngest member of a famous Gypsy troupe that had settled in Montreuil. He'd just been released from La Santé, the prison where he'd met Nono. At first he made as if to not see us. But 10 minutes later, Nono whispered to me:

— Take a look.

A 10-year-old kid was hiding behind a colonnade, keeping an eye on us: the guy had sent him to check on us, to see if we were out looking for him. Typical Gypsy!

You didn't play games with these characters. They're operators from the age of 10...

Nono and I, we did everything together. The next week he took me to his recording studio near Place de Clichy. He was crazy about music and had all these rappers he was supposedly going to finance. In fact, the studio was basically a drug hangout where you had everything under the sun: hashish, ecstasy, cocaine... The ground floor, with concert posters, was sort of okay, but in the basement studio... you needed a flashlight, the smoke was so thick, you could barely move. You've got rap music blaring, go in there and you find a bunch of black men in baseball caps smoking joints, lines of cocaine on the table, it's the rap life all the way. Everybody's high, liquor flows like water, and chicks everywhere. Nono shows me the few albums he'd financed, all flops. On the cover of one of them, a rapper foolishly brandishes his guns. Fuck if they don't look to be the same three assault rifles he showed me before... Seeing them, I made a face.

— Don't matter. Everybody thinks they're fake.

— You're out of your mind. Real guns on an album cover...

Nono was crazy about weapons. He took me to a shooting range. Where? On the Champs-Élysées near Avenue Montaigne, in a private club with an armory. In the basement, there was a shooting range for members. There was an impressive variety of arms: .44 Magnum, micro-Uzi, a Ruger... I couldn't believe it! Here on the Champs-Élysées, one of the busiest streets in the world, and we're practicing with combat weapons. Nono was perfectly relaxed, he went there every day.

—Shooting a couple of hundred rounds makes me feel good!

A genuine nut.

A few days later, I went to see him at his place in Courbevoie.

— Tomorrow I've got to pick up my Israeli buddy at Roissy, I said. Come with?

Nono wanted to introduce me to guy who was eager to be in on a heist. So we made a plan go to the airport to pick up my friend, then get together afterward. Nono and I were going to meet at Opéra at 6:00 PM. I'm already there when I get a message on my pager. I call him back from a telephone booth on Boulevard des Capucines.

— Nono. What are you fucking doing?

— Doc, look... Yesterday I'm sure I saw pigs tailing you...

— What the fuck are you talking about?

— I'm telling you, there's a Safrane with tinted windows...

— Cut the crap...

But at this point, I turn and through the door of the telephone booth I see a blue Safrane. Tinted windows...

Shit! I'm unarmed. I've got nothing. I ask Nono: What's the license plate?

— 92.

That's the one!

— So why are you fucking telling me only now?

— I just woke up 30 minutes ago!

He sometimes slept all day.

— So now what the fuck am I supposed to do?

— Get out of there. Run...

— *Sure, run.* In this neighborhood? With four dicks chasing me? I don't even know what they look like. You must be nuts...

Suddenly the Safran headed directly toward me. I wondered what these cocksuckers were up to. Slowly, a window opened — and I saw Nono... He screamed:

— *Rebenga!*

Like Al Pacino calling to his friend Tony in *Scarface*.

— Crazy bastard! You need help.

— Come on, Rebenga. Get in the fucking car!

He was high as a kite. He must have taken a bunch of drugs before coming to get me. The way he barreled off in the car, I would have put on three seat belts if I could... I don't know why the hounds didn't come after us. Rap music blared, joints in the ashtray, another 20 in a Marlboro box — and not the usual kind but *seum*: smoke one of these joints and sleep for three days. Nono wore two headsets, had two cell phones, and was dressed in combat fatigues.

We drove back up rue Lafayette toward Gare du Nord. As we approach Max-Dormoy metro, Nono shouts: I'm *hungry*. Come with me.

— Not this fucking fast food shit! It's disgusting.

But we get out anyway. Nono has only wads of cash. He orders a meal, then another, then asks what I want. A milkshake. The guy brings the order, places the bags beside the cash register. Nono asks for another meal. And when the guy goes to get it, he grabs the bags. Of course, I follow him out. In the car he bursts into laughter:

— We fucked them, *fucked* them!

Tupac Shakur blaring, smoke from joints, and bags of food, we take off. He drove like a maniac on the highway, then suddenly cut the engine. Not on the shoulder or in the emergency lane: in the middle of the fucking highway. Cars roared past us on either side.

Nono calmly rolled a joint.

— You're freaked out, no?

— I love you, my brother, I replied. Truly. You make me laugh. But get us out of here or we're going to die.

He starts the car and we finally reach the airport. I want to get out but Nono refuses to park the car.

He prefers tooling around the short-term parking lot. We had to wait an hour for my friend's flight, so Nono circles the lot 10 times... At last, my friend's plane lands. From the terminal we walk to the car. Nono's on the phone and starts the car while talking:

— Did you get in touch with the lawyer, Baby? What did he say is going on with him?

We don't say a thing. Nono cuts the music. This must be serious.

— Baby, you know, he's losing it. He's got to get out of there. I stopped to see him yesterday. He's in bad shape, he's going to lose his mind. He can't take it anymore: they've got him in solitary. The lawyer's got to do something. What did that judge do? I've got to write her. Tell you what, I'll drop by to see the judge. The lawyer's got to intervene. Solitary, he can't take it, he's really not well.

He hung up, very upset. He ripped off his headset and threw it out the window.

— Fuck, they're busting my balls. I'm fed up. Breakout! We're going to spring him!

He shoots along the A1 like a madman and the last thing I want is to disturb his concentration. He starts screaming again:

— *Fuck,* I've had it. We're going to help him escape. *Breakout!*

My buddy and I look at each other. What's this all about? I end up saying to Nono:

— You want to get him out of prison — but hold on. Maybe the lawyer's not any good, maybe it's nothing serious. What's the story, who is this guy?

— It's Pattaya.

— Who? What? Pattaya?

— You know. Sure you do. Pattaya, my dog.

— Your *dog* ???

Not to be believed...

— He's in jail, he's considered high-risk, and they've got him in isolation. The judge, that bitch, put him in solitary confinement...

It was too much, I could hardly breath, weeping with laughter. My Israeli buddy was struck dumb, astonished, couldn't believe it. I finally managed to calm down.

— Tell us the story, bro.

— It's just like I fucking said. He's flipping out. They put him in solitary after taking his DNA...

We're tooling down the highway at 200 km per hour, a thick cloud of hashish... and there, Nono le Barge tells us the story of Pattaya:

— We were on the Champs-Élysées, I got to the traffic circle at the Étoile and turned down Avenue de la Grande-Armée. Suddenly this guy fucking cuts right in front of me. So we stopped and exchanged words. We got out of our cars ready to get scrappy... I was ready to fry them. Pattaya was with me. He was in the car and wanted out, too. I told him: 'No, Pattaya, this kickup is between me and them. It's not your business.' But goddamnit, he's *zehef*, very pissed and upset that he's not allowed to take part. Then one of the guys started to run away. Pattaya jumped right through the window and ran the fucker down. And bit him. The other guys freaked out... Then what do you know? The BAC shows up.

— And so?

— Pattaya is jumping up and down. I can't get hold of him. '*Pattaya! Calm down.*' Can't fucking restrain him...

— Why was he so upset?

— He can't stand the pigs. That's because they kill-ed his brother, Ghetto. They put 18 bullets in him!

At that I thought I'd die of laughter.

— And now what's going on?

— He's in the dog pound at Aubervilliers. He's act-ing crazy and they put him in this special section. But we're going to spring him!

— Better to not go batshit.

— We'll see about that! Let's go, come with me. I got visitation rights...

— For a dog?

And yeah, in fact, he needed authorization from the judge.

When we got there, the place looked like a vet-erinary clinic. At reception, phones were ringing and people were waiting for their animals. There were guards.

Nono introduced himself.

— I'm here to see Pattaya...

Total silence, then murmurs. What were they say-ing? Do they think he's some kind of monster?

Somebody from the pound came out:

— You're here to see Pattaya?

— I'm his owner.

Just like Nono said, we're taken to a special sec-tion for dangerous dogs — pit bulls, rotts, shepherds...

We go down a hallway like in *Silence of the Lambs*. We arrive in front of Pattaya's cage. He was a Rottweiler. A beast. Just looking at him, you break out in a cold sweat...

Pattaya, as soon as he sees Nono, he jumps up and bangs into the cage. *Bam!* He takes a couple of steps back and leaps. *Re-bam!* I flip out and hope he won't come shooting out the door. He looks like he's made of steel. He's like out of some comic book. Nono slips a hand through the bars and caresses him.

— Come see Papa. My baby.

The employee quietly comes up to me, nervous.

— The dog is too dangerous. We've got to put him down.

Nono later confessed that he'd put crack in Pattaya's food and blew smoke from joints up the dog's nose... In fact, he'd destroyed the dog's brain. When he talked about the dog, he never called him "my dog." It was always "my son."*

— Pattaya's my boy!

And he really believed it.

When we left the pound, I realized that this guy was both reckless *&* unpredictable.

The next day, Nono called me and I drove to Courbevoie, parked outside and took the elevator up to his apartment. Outside in the hallway, I heard gunshots. The door wasn't locked; I went in. Following

---

* Nono in fact had a son whom he cherished; but with his family he was always discreet and respectful. [Note by J P.]

the noise I came to a bedroom with a massive home theater. Nono sat watching *Heat*... He was dressed in combat fatigues, a balaclava rolled up over his forehead, a bulletproof vest, an M16 in hand, with an automatic pistol inside a gun sock.

— Yo, Nono. What are you doing?

— Getting ready for the job...

We went into the living room to talk. Nono kept preening in front of a giant mirror. Suddenly he grabbed the M16 and aimed it at his reflection...

Fuck if he couldn't make you laugh even as you realized he was mad and crazy and dangerous. But he earned my esteem. I had great respect for him because even if he was nuts, he was tough and determined. He would never squeal, even though he'd had lot of trouble and many clashes with guys in the projects. He was reliable and motivated. Feeling and affection were what motivated him more than anything. With me he always got along, but you were in serious trouble if he didn't like you.

That's the way the criminal environment works in the projects. They know who's who. They keep an eye on everything. When Nono and his partner met me, they trusted me from the get-go. Just as an example, they brought me to their apartment in the 16th...

The 16th arrondissement?

They had a hideout there on Avenue Versailles: 104 m³ with a Porsche in the underground garage.

Nono & his friend offered me another apartment for my personal use if I was on the run. At the time, though, that reminded me of a similar offer from an older hoodlum who lived in the southern banlieue. I'd refused. Why? Because I knew that there was a a feuj, a woman named France, who rented apartments to gang members. I was afraid the place might not be safe. When detectives go after somebody, the first thing they look to is the real estate agency, and all the other apartments that they rent.

So I pulled a little trick. — Sure, an apartment, I said. Is it France you rent it through?

They stared at me.

Yeah — France... You know her?

Yeah, I know her. But I've already got a crib, thanks.

Here, I was just protecting myself. Now they tell themselves: he already has an apartment through France, which reinforces their thinking that I'm feuj myself. Because they don't know my last name, they don't know I'm a beur.

Even Nono?

Yeah, even Nono. I didn't tell him I'm rebeu. I said I was a feuj but understand Arab and speak Hebrew. To mislead them, I once even took them to a kosher restaurant on rue du Faubourg-Montmartre. I wore a yarmulke and Star of David and spoke Hebrew. Like Richard Anconina in *Would I Lie to You?* * Before go-

---

* *La Vérité si je mens!*, a 1997 film directed by Thomas Gilou that recounts the sentimental and comedic adventures of Eddie, a non-Jew trying to pass as Jewish despite his being entirely ignorant of Jewish traditions.

ing, I asked the owner to pretend I was his nephew. He came over when we sat down.

— Drop by tonight to see your aunt.

— No problem. See you tonight, Uncle.

When Nono and his partner saw that, they had no doubts. — The guy who goes after the trucks is a feuj.

But that's all they knew. They would have liked to learn who I'd worked with but I said nothing. I remained a mystery... because I know tomorrow they could talk. Not to give me up, they'd never do that. But with other thugs, they always jabber. At the very least, they talk shit and gossip. For instance, I told them I had a wife and two kids. Cops investigating me will be misinformed. In the end, they didn't even know I was a wanted man. They thought I looked super legit, which was preferable.

Aside from the apartment, were there other proofs of trust?

I brought them into a kind of operation they knew nothing about. Until then they had just been dealing drugs and settling scores, but not armed robbery. Since I was bringing them into my business, they wanted me to get a piece of theirs.

Nono offered me a golden opportunity.

— How about *zetla*? Three or four hundred kilos?

He would give me a super low price. I turned him down but knew a guy in Creil who might be interested. He had 350,000–400,000 francs to spend. I proposed that he make a deal with them where he'd give me the money and I'd pass it along. But Nono's partner didn't want to let go of the merchandise. He tried to con me. Why? Because he was a real thug from the projects. Only his hardcore inner circle was important to him. Everybody else was a loser and a sucker. Fuck them in the ass. If you can rip them off, fine. If you have to smoke them, go ahead. Gang jealousy is lethal. At first they're all hugs & kisses, and they know how to build you up. But shine a little too brightly, and their fucked-up complexes get the upper hand. And that kind of thing can go very, very far. They have a serious issue with other people's success. They're potential psychopaths & can spew forth a pure culture of hate. Even if you're straight-ahead, can be trusted, are not a snitch and have all the tralala to make a perfect delinquent, eh well, if you're surrounded by jealous types, they'll rip you off, take everything you've got… Even kill you. I'm not telling you that there are no rules of the road, but it's more my way or the highway. If a normal person has a problem, you argue and basta. These guys don't live in the same world. They handle conflicts with a Kalashnikov. Thugs in the projects respect only one law, which is their own. Among them there's always a balance of power. They don't like people stepping on their toes. If provoked they can be unpredictable and there's no telling what can happen. Look back at the gang wars in Clos Saint-Nazaire in Stains, or in the projects in Grenoble.*

---

* Reference to a long-running internecine gang war with numerous executions & reprisals in housing projects in the city of Stains.

But Nono has real affection for me even though for him I'm feuj. Which goes to show that with hoods & thugs there's no barriers of race or religion. Only good guys on one side and assholes & motherfuckers on the other. For Nono I was among the best and bravest. So he went to see his friend:

— You're fucked up. Nothin' doin'. Give him his money back. He's a good guy. Nothin' doin'.

The guy was surprised to see Nono take my side, and he was a little afraid of him, too. So everything worked out & my bond with Nono only got stronger.

As Nono and I talked, one thing led to another and we talked recent prison breaks. Nono confided:

— You know the guy whose name is all over the papers? Well, we're the ones who've been taking care of him...

I was in Israel when the guy in question escaped during a transfer to the hospital at Corbeil. I'd read the newspaper account. Just a short article because it was a small-time thug from one of the projects. I didn't know him. At the time I thought he was Portuguese.

Nono told me that, no, he was a dago. He'd provided him with a place to stay, a little cash, and false papers.

The guy wanted to work, and Nono offered to introduce us.

So we met one day in a shopping center. The guy was rather good-looking, short but well-built. Later I'd discover he was something of a hothead, but for now he seemed to me calm and serious.

After we talk a while, I ask him if he's interested in armed robbery. He told me that he was.

We soon developed a complicity. We spoke the same language. We wanted to go after armored trucks, not go to prison, and get a lot of money. He knew about the jobs I'd done. The fact that these jobs were carried out without names attached, but the work of a youngster from the projects, was a good thing. It reinforced my prestige. He and Nono were used to dealing with the sort of traditional thugs who looked down on them. But I was willing to let them profit from my experience and the mistakes I'd made. In all humility. Like them, in fact, they are neither contemptuous nor arrogant. For them as for me, we were the best match possible.

So we decided to help one another, the Italian and I, and it worked out well. Sometimes I slept at his place or vice versa. But like with Nono, I didn't reveal too much about myself. With these people, you can't get too involved. You don't want them to know where you live. Or who you really are. They can end up yapping, and you might do the same. It would be better to avoid working with them altogether, but I had no choice. Their expertise was extremely valuable in terms of planning and logistics, weapons, and overall resources. I brought them together to rob armored trucks and they provided the means: assault rifles, stolen cars, explosives, rocket launchers...

And what did you do together?

Nothing.

That's not what I've been told. Rather, you suggested to them a ramming attack with a truck, like in *Heat*. And, as it turned out, a Brinks armored truck was attacked in Oise in December 1998. Five guys were involved. It happened on a Thursday evening at 6:00 PM not far from the highway toll booth at Senlis. A car forced the Brinks vehicle to brake over the course of a couple of minutes as a dump truck coming from the opposite direction rammed into it. The cut: a few million francs. No shots fired, nobody wounded. Very professional. For your accomplice the Italian, it was his first such job.

I want to point out that the local investigative unit in Lille took a sample of my DNA when I was in prison, and came up empty…

Two weeks after this attack, everything falls apart.

Cops in Lille were coming after me for heists at banks, cash depots, and for armored truck robberies committed around Creil. The BRB wanted me for armored trucks and also for stealing RAM. Police in Amiens were after me for the jewelry store in Chantilly.

I'd fled the country but was finally arrested on December 28, 1998 in Switzerland.

Tell us about it.

Late September 1998 I returned to France from Israel. As usual, I traveled via Switzerland and intended to fly from Zurich to Geneva. But, problem: that day, there were no domestic flights due to a strike. So I had to pass through customs in Zurich, which I'd never done before. The international airport there is under much tighter security than Geneva. Fortunately, it worked out well.

Once out of the airport, though, I had to reach Geneva. Asking around, I was advised to go to the train station and take a train for France via Germany. Despite a premonition, I opted to do that. I almost missed the train, but it was late and I just made it. There was no room in first class, only in second. Problem was, I was a little too well dressed for second class: it's a car full of losers, misfits, and backpackers. I found a seat as the train started to move & then — *fuck*. German cops raid the train looking for illegal immigrants.

A strike, then a train I should have missed, now customs police. My lucky day. I should have put faith in my paranoia but I was slow to react because I was just back from vacation. Each time, same thing; it's the most dangerous time. You've got to exercise caution while on vacation, keep wary and alert.

The cops took my passport — the same fucking passport that American customs officers had already closely examined, and also in England, by a copper with a magnifying glass. And after I'd passed through security there, three guys from Scotland Yard bombarded me with questions before letting me go. With that passport I've been to South Africa, to Algeria during the wave of terrorism, to Israel, where it was closely scrutinized. I'd used it in countries where security was the tightest in the world — and now this little asshole in his customs cap glanced at it, then retreated into a separate compartment to examine it. He came out two minutes later:

— There is a problem with your passport. You must come with me.

— What problem?

I feigned innocence as best I could, but it didn't work. He brought me into another car with about ten guys: Romanians, Albanians, Kazakhs, *who knows what else*. All handcuffed.

— You're not going to keep me with these people. I'm going to complain to my embassy!

The officer seemed unsure. I protested; I didn't let myself be pushed around. Acting very sure of myself, but remaining diplomatic, I refused to be handcuffed and the guy, my passport in hand, consulted with his superior. Who asked me questions and realized I spoke perfect French. And didn't look like an illegal. But that's exactly what got me into trouble. Instead of seeming offended, I would have been better off posing as a Kazakh or a Mongol... Then they would have taken me to a detention facility, from which it's easy to escape. As it was, they now knew I was a French citizen with false identification — not at all the same thing.

They talked together in German and I heard the words *mafiosi* and *terrorist*. They were clearly going to take my fingerprints and contact Interpol — that was going to be bad. Indeed, they asked me to come with them. The train arrived in Basel. I didn't know it, but it had made a U-turn in order to return to customs on the German-Swiss border.

They wanted to handcuff me. I protested in English & threatened to complain to the embassy. They said I could cover the cuffs with my coat. To spare me shame in front of the other passengers, they offered to allow me to follow them freely to the back of the train. But once there, the customs officer made a huge mistake. I convinced him to let me get out first. The handcuffs made it difficult so I asked him to follow close behind me to catch hold of me if I fell. I stepped down hesitantly and with great care. One step, two steps... then as soon as the tips of my Westons touched the platform — *bang*, I took off like a bullet.

Sprinting, I gave it everything I had. Other customs officers were also coming down onto the platform, so I jumped down onto the tracks and I ran. Ahead of me, a train was slowly coming into the station. In a single leap I pulled myself up onto the opposite platform. The approaching train would soon put me out of sight of my pursuers. But it wasn't exactly my lucky day. Cops on the platform onto which I'd jumped — three German guys — started chasing me when they saw me running handcuffed. I ran as fast as I could but then came to a dead end — a 30-foot drop to another platform. I stepped over a barrier but gauging the distance, got scared. Six feet down there was a metal beam but it wasn't even a foot wide... The customs officers were hot on my heels. One of them, a real hulk at least six feet tall, yelled something in German and the tone was: *You're screwed!* I wasn't going to surrender. Still in handcuffs, I dropped onto the beam. I fell squarely onto it with both my feet. Now I had luck on my side. I sat down, then dangled from the beam. Below, it was still 20 feet to the ground. I let go and jumped. More bad luck. I thought my ankle snapped. The pain was incredible. I'd fucked up my foot.

But with a limp I kept going. Cops on the platform above were helpless, yelling and screaming at me to stop. I felt like it was straight out of *The Great Escape*. In Tel Aviv, I'd watched that movie 10 times. I also bought the original soundtrack *&* listened to it over *&* over... Now it was my turn to be handcuffed in a train station and chased by the Germans. It was a movie.

I tried to jump into a car that was stopped at a red light, but the guy sped off. I managed to climb onto a streetcar. Like Jason Bourne in *The Bourne Identity*. I was dripping sweat. Two passengers noticed the handcuffs and like good Swiss citizens, they went to tell the driver. I didn't know what was going to happen. I waited for the next stop, hoping that the bastard was going to open the doors. And he does! I hop out and hobble off, taut as a bow. The passengers watched —but, hey, I grew up in Barbès. I knew about pickpockets from the 18th arrondissement and shoplifted from department stores when I was six years old. I broke into places, went after banks, jewelry stores, and armored trucks. Let them watch all they want. Crime is my life.

I hid inside the entrance to a building, waiting for the streetcar to leave. Then a little further. I made it to the service entrance at the back of a hotel. I went inside, took the elevator to the third floor. The doors to the rooms were almost all open, a maid was cleaning them. I got into one and hid under the bed. I waited. I got my breath back. I didn't move. The pain was terrible in my foot and also my wrists because of the handcuffs. After three hours, I let myself get a drink of water in the bathroom, then went back under the bed. A few minutes later, somebody came in the room. It was a hotel employee. When he left, I had a surge of paranoia. Had he seen me? I decided to get out. But before leaving, I tried to find out where I was. I had no idea. I saw some kind of telephone book that in fact was the brochure for the Mövenpick Hotels in Switzerland. I was in Basel but I tore out the page for Lausanne. Like an idiot, I was certain that I was in Lausanne.

You didn't notice it was written in German, not French?

No, I don't know! I went downstairs to the reception desk. With my coat hiding the handcuffs. But, as I was well-dressed, it went well. I noticed that you needed coins for the telephone booth but I had only 100-dollar bills. I managed to set one down without her noticing the cuffs, and I asked for change. But when she put down the money, I couldn't pick it up. So I pretended to be interested in a promotional poster on the wall behind her. I asked her a couple of questions in English, and while she turned to look at the poster, I quickly scooped up the change.

I went to a phone booth and called a contact in Tel Aviv.

— Bro', you've absolutely got to call our good pal in Strasbourg.

— And say what?

— Tell him he's got to come pick me up. I'm in some bad shit. It's crazy.

I explained the situation. He started to flip out.

— Okay, I'll call.

I managed to enter the rooftop terrace of the hotel where there was a swimming pool. On the street, I saw cop cars zooming around looking for me. An hour later I went down to the phone booth to call my contact again. He gave me the phone number of a friend. I called.

— Come right away, I'm in Lausanne. Near the Mövenpick Hotel. There's a square, I'll be hiding there...

The guy takes his motorcycle, went by way of Mulhouse, near Basel, and races to Lausanne, 30 miles away. *Lausanne.* I stayed the whole night beside the hotel without seeing the guy. It was fortunate that I didn't stay in the hotel because cops searched it all night long.

In the morning, leaving the square, I asked a passerby where I was.

— Basel!

What the fuck… I called my friend back to tell him.

— I made — uh, a mistake.

— What?

— I'm not in Lausanne. I'm in Basel…

— Just got back. I'll leave right away.

At exactly that moment, I turned around to find 20 cops, standing in front of the booth.

— That's okay, bro'. Too late, I'm dead…

He understood I was nailed. I hung up.

The cops brought me to the commissariat of the police in the Basel train station. They explained that they were going to turn me over to the German authorities since they were the ones who arrested me in the first place. I complained about my ankle and asked for a wheelchair, telling them I couldn't walk. The hulk of a cop from the day before harshly slapped me in the face… We glared at each other. He put me in a cell, a lousy cell, full of down-and-outers like you never saw, even in Algeria. It was out of *Midnight Express*. Kurds, Albanians, all illegals, all depressed. They'd spent all their money to emigrate only to be sent back to their shitty countries.

I was going to try to sleep. A detective came in, yelling and waving at me to come out. He grabbed me by the shoulders and yelled some more. He was upset because I'd escaped. Then came four more detectives. One of them spoke excellent French.

— You were in Israel?

Now of course, I'm going to lie.

— In Be'er Sheva.

— What were you doing there?

— I was visiting Jewish friends from Paris.

— Why are you carrying a fake passport?

— I'm illegal, from Algeria.

I gave the name and date of birth of a cousin of mine who lived in our little village in Algeria. They took my fingerprints.

— Since you entered Germany illegally, you'll have to pay a $500 fine.

— Okay.

— And we're transferring you to Swiss authorities.

They took a deposition and then made note of my injury. At that point, they turned themselves into nurses from the International Red Cross… I still didn't realize I had a fractured heel, & a hematoma. These German cops brought me something to drink, to eat, and treated me with great consideration. They called for a doctor, then turned me over to the Swiss.

And no sooner had the Germans left that one of the Swiss police punched me in the face. He blurted with disdain, "Germans are really stupid."

— Why?

— Handcuffing you in front. Behind-the-back is the way they should do it. Always.

And with that, they brought me to the hospital. I waited for an X-ray while in a wheelchair. A cop offered to buy me something to drink and when he went to the vending machine, I mulled things over. I was in too much pain to think of running. I had to try to steal his gun. It was an old-fashioned pistol stuck in an unattached holster with a belt clip.

In Israel, I'd practiced Krav Maga with my weapons specialist buddy. The purpose of this martial art is defensive: to disarm your adversary. And the first thing you learn is to move lightning fast in order to arm yourself. I'd done it dozens of times but wondered if I'd have time enough to get his gun out of the holster.

That day, there was a highway traffic accident, and emergency rooms were overwhelmed. So, no time for my X-ray. The cops decided to take me to jail, saying they'd bring me back the next day. That would give me another chance. They drove me to the Basel so-called penitentiary.* I almost expected to run into the Dalton gang inside. Within the jail itself they've got a police station. Just try to escape!

Once in my cell, I peeled off the bandage to slow the healing. I told myself I must stay in the hospital as long as possible. But then I had an idea — that I was making a mistake. On the contrary, I should keep my bandage on and let it heal so as to be in the best possible shape. Then, tomorrow, I'd pretend to be in pain.

The next day, my foot was still so swollen that I couldn't put my shoe on. I hid it in the pocket of my overcoat, which I'd been allowed to keep with me. For half an hour, I practiced disarming the cop. I must have done it 150 times. As I got into shape, my determination came back. I've got to escape today before the French police check my fingerprints and alert the

*   Basel City Deportation Prison.

Swiss that I'm looking at 15 years in prison. Now I'm guarded by just two cops, but as soon as they know that, I'll find myself in solitary confinement.

What I didn't know at the time was that my fingerprints had already arrived in Paris, and the French police were flipping out. Early the next morning they set out to come get me.

After a brief medical exam in the jail, they took me to the hospital. But to get there, unbelievably, they put me on crutches. I recalled that the Swiss cop had told me that prisoners must always be cuffed with hands in back, never in front. And now I didn't have any at all! In the police van, I tried to get a look at the city for an idea of where I was in case there was a chance to escape. Once at the hospital, two cops brought me inside while the third stayed in the van. I walked with great difficulty, putting on an act. I was brought to a doctor in her office. She was racist and, more, she didn't like prisoners. She refused to keep me in the hospital despite my pleas. Tears in my eyes, I made a big show about how I was afraid of prison. Without success. I was due to come back in two weeks.

While a nurse dressed the wound, the cops were waiting for papers. One of them stuck his head in the door to warn me it was almost time to go. As soon as he ducked out, I put my foot on the floor & tried to put weight on it. It was okay. No pain. I took out the shoe I'd kept all along in my overcoat pocket and succeeded in putting it on. I lifted my knee, it was fine.

Now it was time to go. I had to get the gun. I grew determined. I left the office to go with the two cops. I had to keep one of them busy. I handed my file to the cop on my right. Between them, we started for the exit, all three of us, me in the middle. In walking with my crutches, my left hand just about brushed against the cop's gun. They had no clue. Then it was time, and I counted: *one, two…* But then I got scared. On crutches, between two cops, & I didn't know where I was. This would be total improvisation, which I hate. More, I'd made them hunt for me yesterday all over the city. But now I looked up and had a flash the moment I laid eyes on the police van. I had absolutely no desire to go back to prison. *You've got to move. Go, now.* Without another thought I dropped the crutches and grabbed the gun off the cop to my left. I moved so fast I wonder if he even noticed. The other one, slightly ahead of me and holding my medical records, didn't see a thing. But they both reacted to the crutches falling. Luckily, I'd managed to get the gun before they'd clattered to the ground.

I turned to the one cop and gave him a violent blow with one elbow. I hit him so hard I thought he might be badly hurt. He was not unconscious but he was down. I stole his gun, a SIG Sauer. I went to cock it but there was a bullet already in the chamber! It almost jammed. The other cop ran to the van and was already on the phone sounding the alarm. I took off in the opposite direction, running faster and faster down the hallway. Super! Outside the hospital I see this little camionette with its hazard lights flashing. The driver is pretty clearly looking for directions.

Luck was now definitely on my side.

— *Hey — you lost?*

— *Ja...*

You'll see if you're lost; I'm going to help you find your way!

I made him get in and take the wheel, and I attached his seatbelt for him to keep him from trying to run. I spoke to him in English.

— *See this gun? I'm dangerous...*

The guy freaked out but he started the car. Meanwhile, a police car was backing up and two cops in bulletproof vests jumped out. They took shotguns out of the trunk and ran toward the hospital.

So, I think to myself: *Hey, bro'! You've just disarmed a cop and have a gun. You've escaped the police for the second time in 24 hours. Don't fucking head for the border. Don't try to go by way of Mulhouse.*

— To the highway!

But the guy was already on the way to the train station — where the customs officers had grabbed me in the first place! But in fact the highway was nearby, and no toll booth. Reading a sign, I was 250 miles from Geneva. I pressured the driver:

— *Geneva! Quick! Get me there fast & you'll be free.*

I asked if he had a wife and children. He said no. I asked where his parents lived.

— They're dead.

Fuck!

I grabbed his wallet and inside found a photo. Of a dog.

— *What's this?*

— *Please, please — don't touch my dog... Please, please...*

I made him understand that, if he did anything stupid, I'd butcher his mutt. His dog, it was like a son to him — another Pattaya... He was just as crazy as Nono. But straight.

When we reached Geneva, I let the guy go off in his pick-up truck. I went to a phone booth and called my buddy.

— It's me, bro'.

He thought this must be a movie. I told him how I'd disarmed the cops after spending a night in jail. That I'd made it to Geneva but my foot was in terrible pain. I gave him a place to meet in the garden of Eaux Vives Park, facing Leman Lake. We knew the place well because we used to go to a restaurant in the Park.

— I'll be there. Tonight.

I didn't leave the park until he arrived. I was worn out and wrecked. Except, there, my hands weren't cuffed and I had a gun. *Nothing bad can happen to you.* When you've done dozens of robberies and you're good with guns, the assurance you get from a pistol is crazy. It's not the fact you can kill somebody, but simply the pressure and power you can exert over people. You're in your element.

Finally, hours later, my friend came. After he picked me up, instead of immediately getting back on the highway, we decided to stop in a hotel to get some rest. While he checked in, I stayed in the car.

No upside in drawing attention. To rejoin him in the room on the top floor, I took the elevator from the underground parking garage. Once we locked the door, it was beautiful. A superb jacuzzi, and there was everything on the menu, from champagne to petits-fours. But I felt so comfortable in the jacuzzi that I didn't have the strength to eat.

— Life's insane...

— Why?

— A little more than 24 hours ago, I was in the slammer, looking at many years of confinement. I was in some international deep shit. But I took destiny in my hands and, barely a day later, here I am with you. Relaxing.

Next day, we crossed the border and drove toward Annecy. Not even a customs officer in the booth. Once in Annecy, we took the highway back to Paris.

After that incredible escape, you went back to Paris. Didn't you think the police were on high alert and would do everything to capture you?

What I didn't know was that not one but several police forces were on my ass: the BRB, but also the OCRB,* the BRI,† and especially the SRPJ‡ in Lille, which

---

* *Office central pour la répression du banditisme*, or Central Bureau for the Repression of Banditry.

† *Brigade de Recherche et d'Intervention*, or Research & Intervention Brigade, with a focus on gangs.

‡ *Service régional de police judiciaire*, a branch of the national police force.

was following up every lead. The Lille pigs in the office at Creil were the most dangerous. They worked almost full time on my case. These fuckers were very obstinate. Some cops are totally obsessed with hunting down outlaws. I stay away from Oise in order not to alert them. For a thief like me, those cops are to be avoided like the plague. I keep a low profile in the Parisian scene.

The French police had already spent three years looking for me. Now they believed that they finally nailed me. I can just picture their faces when they arrived in Switzerland to be told, "Hey, sorry. He's gone..." When I was later arrested, the BRB, the PJ, and the whole French police force, all of them would tell me:

— Fuck, in Switzerland, you put on a helluva show.

It was like they didn't care anymore about the armored truck robberies or bank heists, or anything else.

— You're crazy, I kept telling them. — That wasn't me in Switzerland...

I denied everything. One day, a cop with the BRB said to me:

— The Swiss police would like to get their Sig Sauer back. Do you know what you did with it?

— I threw it in a lake somewhere...

He started to fill out a police report. — I'm listening. Are you serious?

— It's all bullshit.

He tore up the report, telling me that bullshit costs taxpayers' money.

What if I told him how much my escape cost me?

Once back in Paris, what did you do?

I took care of myself. At an orthopedic pharmacy I bought a special shoe for my foot. I consulted the same doctor who'd taken care of my gunshot wound. He treated me; all went well.

The OCRB devoted whole confabs to me. The judge later told me:

— You weren't Public Enemy Number One, but you were the most sought-after criminal in Paris and Île-de-France.

It was quite true that big names heard about me when they were questioned in custody. Cops want to know about a guy goes by the name Doc, real name Rédoine Faïd, wounded in the robbery at Villepinte. These guys send word that I might be seriously dangerous since the entire BRB was on my tail.

How did they finally get you ?

When I was arrested in Switzerland, I had an airline ticket purchased from a Parisian travel agency around Faubourg-Montmartre. The BRB located the agency thanks to careful work by the Lille SRPJ in Creil. They asked the employee there to alert them if I showed up. And in fact, sometime after that, a friend purchased tickets for me. On December 28, I went to pick them up. I drove there in a little Twingo with one of Nono's partners and the Italian guy. I automatically asked them to drop me a short distance from the travel agency to keep from being seen together. The Italian was also a wanted man.

It's a winter evening. It's dark. The street is busy. The cops who've been watching me for the past few days think they spot me going into the place but they aren't sure. After a few minutes I come out, but the friend who was supposed to pick me up hasn't arrived yet. I go shopping. When I enter a perfume store just across the street from Le Palace, a nightclub, the plainclothes detectives are able to positively identify me.

They must have recognized me through the store window. They're with the armed robbery division of the BRB, and have been after me for three years. Now they see me in person for the first time. They must be thinking that if they don't nab me right now, they might not see me for another 10 years. My friend arrives. Not noticing anything strange, I come out of the store and walk to the car.

Just as I get in, a Renault Laguna cuts us off in front, a Volkswagen stops beside, and a Safrane behind. The sidewalk is full of pedestrians.

As the Laguna jams into reverse, a cop rushes out, revolver in hand. He's an old geezer from the 1960s. But he's got balls. He rushes at me to make the arrest. He and his partners don't know if I'm armed, and they freak out.

Use force when arresting dangerous suspects only if necessary... You've got to be kidding. Bullshit. I get my face smashed in. Even lying on the ground and cuffed, they punch me over and over and destroy my face. These aren't television cops like Navarro or Julie Lescaut. They're not psychologists who play nice with suspects. It's more along the lines of: *You dirty bastard cock-sucking sonofabitch.*

I stayed quiet.

Behind me, another one with a huge pistol, who looks like Nick Nolte:

— You're unarmed? Too bad. I was hoping to waste you...

I'm loaded into the Laguna. The driver is a young guy & obviously has worked my case hard. He drives, gun in hand, and tells me:

— Rédoine, you bat an eye, I swear I'll put a bullet in your brain...

Another cop aims his pistol directly at my head. We're driving fast through Paris traffic and I'm afraid the gun will go off by accident. I sense they're under tremendous pressure. They must have built me up into a terrible legend. What had gone down in Switzerland traumatized them. They take me to be truly dangerous.

Once at the prefecture, they force me to hobble up the stairs. I could still feel their sense of panic. Usually they bring you downstairs to take your picture. In my case, somebody from the identification bureau came to my cell. They asked if I wanted to see a doctor. I refused.

— You don't want to see the doc or file a complaint about the pounding you just got?

— No, it's okay.

They were surprised.

— Fuck, this guy doesn't even want to see the doctor.

The interrogation begins. They've typed up a chart with the names of all the big gangsters they've traced to the 93rd. One of the cops, who'd investigated the Postiches gang, can't stand guys like me from the banlieue. For him and a lot of cops like him, the clever thief can only be a Gaul from Marseilles or Corsica. Surely not a little Arab from the projects. Consequently, they imagine I must be second fiddle to more serious criminals. There were some braggarts, four or five guys from the 93rd who'd carried out an attack far less brilliant than ours, and they'd prattled on about having done a job with us, using other people's work to make themselves look good. As a result, they ended up in prison.

The detectives had their doubts about these guys and handed me the police report. I didn't even look at the transcript. I wouldn't sign anything and didn't say a word. They undressed me and performed a body search, and left me naked in front of my friend, a woman who'd been arrested with me. A despicable attempt to humiliate me, as if I'd robbed somebody's mother or father. They seemed to take it personally. The guy who'd threatened me during the arrest came in while I was handcuffed and lying naked on the floor. He kicked me hard in the back.

— Oh, sorry. I didn't see you...

What's with this crazy asshole?

Another cop showed me my photo:

— Now I can take this off my desk... I'm sick of looking at it the past three years.

They bring me back to my cell block, where there's an old police chief who must be in his 60s, and he sits smoking a pipe. He says:

— You don't know me, Faïd, but I know you...

I say nothing.

— Three years is long enough. It had to stop. Now we've got you. I wanted to look you in the eye.

And he walks away.

A group from the BRB arrived three hours later. They'd been waiting for me at the airport. They bring me out of my cell.

— Champagne! We're going to take a group photo with you.

In fact, they never did. But I could feel how super-satisfied they were with themselves, and I would've liked to bring them down a notch. Because I never killed anybody; I don't have blood on my hands. I'm not another Mesrine.

One of them takes me back, accompanied by two guards. Still handcuffed, I'd stay that way the whole time with the BRB.

— You're not a talker, you.

I didn't even answer. They realized by now that I won't say a thing. Not a word. I know I'm going to do time and wonder what prison I'll be in. I don't want to go to Fresnes, my brother's already there. But just the same, it's where I end up. A tough place with squealers and stool pigeons. But I know the scene. An older convict gave me the lowdown.

While waiting to be transferred, they mock my lawyer, a big name in criminal justice.

— He's going to come here, that big-mouthed gasbag.

If they don't like him, he must be good. It means he gets guys out. He wins cases.

They question me a second time. Same deal. One of them hands me a police report asking if I know this guy or that. I don't even look. I don't know anybody. The Nick Nolte character, the one who'd kicked me when I was on my back, talks to me while typing on the computer, and at first I can't figure him. He reeks of contempt for criminals. I wonder why he's so aggressive, so violent and vindictive. But it's the result of wading through the swamp. Pigs themselves start to feel a kind of disgust.

I don't mean to defend him. But I have to say that later on, after being in prison, I'll come to realize that criminals are really rotten. They're guys who have sex with their friend's wife when their friend's doing time — and they don't even help them. You're talking about guys who aren't straight about sharing, psychopaths who beat you to a pulp for next to nothing. You can admire thieves who do the right thing in prison or out, but those types are very, very few. The ones who are on the up and up, who don't talk shit, I won't fucking lie to you, are very few. Beautiful guys who greet their friends with an envelope full of cash when they get out of prison, who've taken care of their parents, their wife and kids — these are few and far between. Most of the time, criminals who do well in prison do it on their own dime.

So Nick Nolte types, putting up with all this — with guys who talk big when he's interrogating five or six of them together but who get scared when they're one-on-one — can only come away disgusted. They've got the records and know that a guy doesn't act in prison the same when being interrogated. He weeps, he begs his wife to come visit him — & be sure to bring some hash... They start to see these guys as total shits and they're not entirely wrong.

These cops didn't start out that way. Probably they started out with preconceived ideas about grand larceny and dashing criminals, big important cases...

Moreover, cops like these can't have much of a family life. They go through a couple of lousy divorces, don't even know their kids. The job eats them alive, even when you sense their passion for the work. But to me, none of that makes me have any sympathy for them.

This particular day, though, what pisses them off is having to deal with me — a 25-year-old Algerian instead of a nice French boy... They can't stand lousy North Africans who stick to their guns & keep their mouths shut. Even more, they don't understand how a fucking rebeu from the projects can go to Tel Aviv via Geneva with a terrific looking fake passport.

It's obvious they can't imagine how beurs like us can be so organized and professional... They clearly take me to be a novice. In the van, as they transport me to the tribunal at Créteil, Nick Nolte tells me about one beur from the 93rd who they almost caught three weeks ago, but he managed get away in his car.

— He's a fast driver, no, wouldn't you say?

— I don't know what you're talking about.

I immediately realized he had a hidden tape recorder. There again, older convicts had warned me: when you're in custody, & particularly while you're being transferred, you're always going to be taped. The recording will be given to the investigating magistrate. That's why Nick Nolte tried to tone things down a notch after treating me like the biggest shit the world had ever known... Why not have a drink together while we're at it?

Obviously, I didn't say a word.

C., who was more adept, asked me: What made you decide to go after armored trucks? What motivated you?

I think to myself: *You really are an asshole. I did this all myself.* He still can't imagine that a beur from the projects could do it alone.

And now, out of rancor, a third guy chimes in:

— When you play games, you've got to know how to lose.

I say nothing.

— You must not be able to stand losing, since you don't confess...

— Maybe it's just a game for you. But not for me. Silence.

— If you don't talk, you know you're going to end up in jail.

— Yeah, I'll do six or seven years. So fucking what? That wasn't the answer he expected.

— Let me tell you something, he replies, angrily, those years are going to cause you nothing but pain.

Be a good sport, in other words. Sure.

What came next?

They bring me in front of the judge. At the Créteil courthouse, they separate me from the other detainees. I realize I'm going to be treated differently. For transport to and from prison, I'm brought separately into the van. Once arrived at Fresnes, everybody is taken out except me. I'm the last one, and I'm escorted by 10 gendarmes who put me in the hands of a dozen screws specially waiting for me in the yard. It was like a changing of the guard. It's true I'd been given two pages in *Le Parisien* and an article in *Libération*. So in their eyes, I'm this huge catch. The newspaper stories came out two days after my arrest. Meanwhile, the BRB police must have been on stakeout at one or two of our hideouts, hoping to nab my partners. They were also following the friend who'd been arrested with me. Unfortunately for them, she knew how to behave and had absolutely nothing to do with my activities. And she knew how to act in case of a problem. She must not see anybody or even step into a telephone booth.

In prison, the guards placed me in solitary confinement.

Your first time in jail?

The very first. The emotional shock is immense. You're not terribly scared because you know you're not exactly going to die, but you have this enormous apprehension. You discover the horrifying truth that you're going to be confined to a cell for years to come.

I'm alone in mine because I'm DPS.* After setting down my bag, my first reflex was to check if I could see outside... Through the wire grille — zilch. Later I'd learn how to use a piece of broken mirror taped onto a toothbrush to see what's happening. For the moment, I just fell asleep. Like anybody after being brought before a judge, knowing that they're in for a long stretch.

They'd put me in Division II, which means a type of solitary confinement, but worse, because you're treated like it's regular incarceration... As a result, you can't say anything. If you're in real solitary, you can go before a committee and ask to be transferred. But here I couldn't because I was treated just as if I was in the general population.

I started to mull things over. How did I get caught? Who had ratted on me? Have they really released my friend? Did they capture the Italian who was with me in the car? I was anxious to see my lawyer.

I finally decided to go out during exercise time. It was like a different world; I felt like an alien from another planet. The cell door opened and I went out. I heard noise in the corridor, guards talking, cell doors opening. In Fresnes, well-known for discipline, everything is based on a kind of mythic notion of psychological conditioning. When the guards come to open your cell, the door is secured with two old-fashioned Vachette locks that clack loudly when opened.

* *Détenus particulièrement signalés*: A high-risk prisoner held in isolation.

— *FAÏD! Walk!*

Authority, discipline. But, the fact is, the guards are terribly afraid of you.

Cells in the second division have double locks. In addition to the cell door, there's a security enclosure with bars. Over time, it's very tough, psychologically. You get the distinct feeling that you're being kept in a cage. Cells in the two other divisions have only one door.

Exercise takes place in a wedge-shaped yard with a grille above your head. The yard is filthy, rat droppings everywhere — I've seen rats as big as cats. And it's cold. A guard watches over me from a sentry box, but he doesn't like to talk.

— This is the yard? I ask. Where are the other prisoners?

— Here you're by yourself. You're DPS.

I'm wearing jeans, a shirt, a leather jacket, loafers. I'm not yet in prison attire.

It's Saturday morning and I receive a change of clothes from my family.

That afternoon, I'm allowed a second walk. This time with company — a lunatic. Prison is full of them. The guards can't control them so they end up in isolation. Which obviously makes them worse and even more violent. And they get more time for having lashed out at guards or other prisoners. They end up doing 10 years even though, when they arrived, they were in for only two or three.

This guy enters the yard and walks toward me.

— You here for rape?

— No man, nothing at all like that.

— I want to tell you something. I'm not normal.

— Okay...

I try to not pay attention. The guy comes back.

— The guards, they're all fucking assholes. I want to whack one. Want to barricade the walk with me?

— What?

— What I mean is *refuse*. Not go back in the cellblock.

I don't know what to say. What the fuck do I care?

— Sure, okay. We'll stay in the yard.

The guy opens his mouth *&* rolls his tongue. Revealing a razor blade.

— If it gets nasty, I'll waste them all.

This guy is over six feet tall. He's a beast. And a moron. So I have to wonder what I'm going to do if he decides to attack me. He could slit my throat in two seconds. Killing another inmate might be the plan he's got to be transferred to another prison.

He comes back to me:

— Forget it. I'm going to see the warden. I'll do the barricade myself right there in his office.

— Okay, good. You do that.

When the door finally opens, I feel a huge sense of relief. My first prisoner encounter.

Weren't you afraid of what might happen the next day?

Next morning, I go out again. No, I don't avoid him because I've got to have fresh air. In prison you have to get out. You need to walk because the ability to move in your cell is so limited. It was the right thing to do. Yesterday's crazy character didn't come back. There's another guy, though. But completely different. Name of Nordine T.

A bank robber, age 40. By smuggling in guns and taking guards hostage, he'd escaped Valence Penitentiary. He went to spring his wife, who was an inmate in a prison nearby, then stole a car and escaped. Before he was caught and sent back to prison, Nordine got to know a fair number of rogues from the southern banlieue and also some big names in Marseilles. Not knowing who I was, he was very much on his guard with me. That was the usual attitude among criminals from the 1980s: trust nobody, don't talk to anybody. It's okay if your past is known, but otherwise, keep your distance. Fresnes during that time was mainly inmates from the banlieue: guys like Riton, Lepage, Émile Dieudonné, Didier Cadet, Francis Schmidt... But that's a bygone era. The yard for DPS prisoners doesn't see great thugs from the past. Today there are young guys, crazies, any number of snitches, and a few crooks.

But Nordine is one of those old-fashioned criminals, who sizes you up right away. These guys have a very specific way of looking at you. So he doesn't ask why I'm here. He asks if I need anything:

— Thanks, I'm good.

But that doesn't stop him from having me sent a package from the canteen. I start to get who he is. Next day I go out in a tracksuit but with street shoes, so I can't really exercise. He passes me a pair of Nikes. They're too small but still. Then flip-flops for the shower. Little by little, he starts to see me as okay. He realizes that for a new inmate, I put up well with confinement. He gets the fact I take authority to be the enemy, and he likes that. He appreciates it that I'm verbal. Evenings he calls me through the windows and we talk. At 8:00 PM, he leaves to go watch the news.

He takes charge of my penitentiary education, like an older brother:

— Neaten up your cell but do it quickly. Your cell must be clean but don't forget: you don't live here. It's not your home. I've been in this place for 10 years but my mind is always on the outside.

And again:

— When the guard says good morning, you only nod. Don't say a word. If he asks how you are, you never ever reply by greeting him. Every day without fail, you go out and take your walk...

Once I managed to get sneakers, we exercised together. Nordine was a fucking athlete with the figure of a Greek statue. I called him Ninja and he nicknamed me Little Samurai.

We played squash against the wall, striking the ball with our hands. I need the exercise but since I'm a DPS, I can't use the sports field. But Nordine warns me:

— If you file a request for access to the weight room or sports field, you'll wait two or three months for authorization. In the meantime you'll already have been transferred out.

OUTLAW

As days go by and we get to be friends, I learn he was an armed robber, that he still has 10 years to go. I tell him that I'm in prison for attacking armored trucks, banks, and jewelry stores. That makes him like me even more.

One morning, a new guy arrives in "our" prison yard. We find it strange that this guy, who was usually assigned to the yard across from us, turns up here. Also, we learn that he's got the same magistrate in Bobigny who's assigned to my armored truck robbery. This guy was in his mid-40s and had spent half his life in the joint. He wasn't doing well and complained all the time. Nordine knew his group and advised me to avoid his company. So as soon as he shows up, we stop talking. Criminal magic: a quick glance and I know not to talk in front of this guy.

Nordine also tells me explicitly: gangsters are almost all bastards.

One day, the guard announces:

— *Faïd, police check.* Proceed to the visiting room.

I call Nordine:

— Police control, visiting room. What's happening?

— Damn, you're being taken directly into custody...

— Call the lawyer and everybody else if I don't come back.

— Okay.

In the visiting room there was a cop from the DRPJ of Versailles.* He was investigating a theft of

---

* *Direction Régionale de la Police Judiciaire.* This arm of the French police had recently created a unit to investigate crimes involving information technology.

memory cards. I'd also have a visit from the SRPJ from Lille, who'd take a sample of my DNA to match that recovered at the site of a robbery in Oise. They were convinced it was me. Nordine later told me I should systematically refuse such visits because I have nothing to say and refuse to sign their reports.

Tell me more about your life in jail.

Six months passed and I still haven't seen my family. I write my sister and my father. I don't understand why they haven't visited. My lawyer asks about it. He learns that the magistrate in Senlis has turned my case into a personal matter and restricted my visitation rights. It's a kind of persecution I don't understand. In the reports she's looking at, there's no violence whatever. We're not talking about heinous crimes. I'm not asking her to admire me, but don't get why she's got a fixation on me and blocks my visits. She must have thought my three years' flight from justice was like a taunt. That wasn't at all the case. But for the moment, I had to suffer; there must be real punishment.

I've had other examining magistrates who were much more on the level. One of them had a poster of *Les Tontons flingueurs* in his office.* He also had a police cap, a *kepi de gendarme* that must have belonged

* A 1963 comedy crime film directed by Georges Lautner. It is an adaptation of the Albert Simonin book *Grisbi or no grisbi* (*Loot or No Loot*). *Tontons flingueurs* literally translates to gun toting uncles.

to his father. Talking with him was like talking to Michel Audiard.* He didn't think like the police. It wasn't because you were Arab that he'd doubt you were a professional: he knew that I was self-taught and there were no big names behind what I was doing. Quite simply because, if I had been involved with big gangsters, the cops would have heard about it. He tried to understand how I got where I was all by myself. He talked with me about sports and movies. I learned later that his nickname was "The Artist." Other inmates would warn me how clever he was.

At first I kept my mouth shut. He tells me:

— You'll see. 18 months *&* you'll change your mind.

But a year and half later, I still don't talk. He made me think he was going batshit. He told his clerk to leave the office and told me:

— Rédoine, we've matched your DNA. You're implicated in this case. You're the key to the puzzle. The clerk's not here. So tell me and it'll be just between you *&* me. It was a perfect attack. What went wrong at the end?

— I don't know what you're talking about...

— Listen, friend. I've been at this job for nine and a half years... He leaned back in his chair. You're one of the toughest.

I realized that in the end, most suspects talk.

Each time I meet with him, he shakes my hand. He gives a little smile of complicity. We always showed

---

* A French screenwriter well-known for witty, slang-infused dialogue.

respect for one another. He probably didn't think highly of me, but he was fair. That was the case with all the judges I dealt with, except the magistrate in Senlis.

She gave me a hard time with no visits for a year. Fortunately, I had Paul and Edith, volunteer prison visitors with big hearts.

During this period, my sister was in a car accident. She barely survived while my three-year-old niece and brother-in-law both died. My youngest nephew was left in a coma. But all of this didn't give me the right to have visitors. No mercy. I'm not going to complain, I guess it's common. An attempt at psychological torture.

After two years the situation changed when the judge was transferred and the case was closed in Senlis. My new examining magistrate was much more humane. She arranged for a familial meeting at the detention center in Villepinte and I could finally see my sister and feel closer to my family.

Meanwhile, after 20 months at Fresnes, I was transferred to solitary confinement at Fleury-Mérogis; this came about as required by the security rotation order for DPS prisoners. Prison administration thought I was planning to escape. Police warned them.

Can I give you their version of that?

I'm listening.

A judiciary police report, more precisely, a communication from the BRB in Paris, had it that in October 2000, you planned an escape from Fresnes with the use of explosives. In 2003, the prisoner Antonio Ferrara would carry out just such an operation, a spectacular event that made national headlines. This report states that you were in touch with Ferrara, an Italian, and with a certain individual named Cohen, an Israeli. At several meetings in Paris, they agreed to the delivery of assault rifles, an RPG-7 rocket launcher, & type C4 explosives in "their plan to help one Rédoine Faïd, a.k.a. 'Doc', escape from the high security section of Fresnes Penitentiary." Cohen, who lived in Tel Aviv, supplied technical and tactical knowledge for the operation. He was a former military man and belonged to the elite corps known as "Tsahal." The BRB report mentions that Cohen served as an instructor in mine-clearing operations.

Any of this ring a bell?

Antonio Ferrara? Like everybody else, I've heard of him. He's supposed to be a good guy and a straight arrow. Courageous to boot! But I never met with him. As to Cohen, I know him quite well and can't deny it. He's a great friend, but I'm not aware of anything he's done that's unlawful. Your question leaves me cold.

Then let me continue. According to BRB investigators, Cohen and Ferrara planned to aid in your escape from a high security prison. But some sort of indiscretion scuttled the operation at the last moment. Which led to your immediate transfer to Fleuris-Mérogis. An international rogatory commission sent two officers of the BRB to Tel Aviv to interrogate Cohen by way of Interpol.

They suspected he was the explosives specialist for the gang that attacked armored vehicles, of which you were the mastermind. What was astonishing is that, despite the scuttled attempt in 2000, Ferrara would use the same method to escape from the isolation cell block at Fresnes in 2003.

If Ferrara succeeded in breaking out of Fresnes, he owes it mostly to guys from the outside who came to help him. Which is proof of his straight-ahead character, because these guys had to be highly motivated to spring him the way they did. As for my so-called plans, nobody ever proved I intended to escape. So far as I know, I never tried any such thing — never sawed through a prison bar.

Eventually you were taken to Villepinte Prison. How did that go?

I was placed in ordinary detention, the same as youngsters from the projects. They had cellphones, cable channels, played soccer, and had the best mess halls of all the Parisian detention centers. They had Halal meals and fridges in their cells. The guards were easygoing. The inmates reigned supreme. It was another world.

When I arrive, my guard there was super-nice. He welcomed me, and immediately contacted social services because they forgot to send my visitation permit. He also offered to call my family. Upright guy. I was very rebellious back then and couldn't stand prison, but now I developed a different relationship with the guards. Maybe it was a strategy on their part, but it was much better. They don't want disorder and chaos, and things went well.

There were fights, of course, some clashes. But it was much livelier than at Fresnes. When the guard would offer to take me to recreation, I was out of my cell as soon as he opened the door. There'd be four or five kids in the activities room, you'd have board games, a ping-pong table. This is a prison? The walls are 30 feet high but there are no bars on the windows. The place is meant for minor offenders: drug dealing and crap like that. Only three of us are DPS: me, Nordine la Gelée, and Gérard, who'd been with the Dream Team.

Were you able to get together with them?

No. We were kept apart, each in a different building. Nordine was generous to a fault. He sent me cigarettes even though I don't smoke. To younger guys he explained who I was, and they came asking me, very respectfully, if I needed anything.

In prison I'd come to know the famous Maghrebian underworld that I'd never been involved with. I'd known their names, meeting places, nightclubs. Nordine la Gelée, Momo A., Ihmed M., Djamel B. from the jewelry store heist at Place Vendôme... I realized that they were all stand up guys.

Djamel, a 45-year-old from Kabyle, whom I'd meet again in the pen at Saint-Maur. He was super cultivated and spent his days in the library. We often played chess & he always beat me. He would have done well in any profession but chose to be a gangster. Another was Mohammed A., a natural prince. Hyper-intelligent and with great poise, he knew everybody. He was a godfather type and would have been an excellent CEO.

In the prison yard, you found all the Venezuelan and Colombian "mules" who'd been arrested at Charles de Gaulle airport. Like good South Americans, they were passionate soccer fans and played against a team from the 93rd. In their games, I'd substitute if they needed a linkman. In the same measure I'd been deprived of everything at Fresnes and Fleury Mérogis, I felt full of life at Villepinte. The games invigorated me and I became great friends with the Latinos. They gave me a taste for their food and I soon started to learn Spanish.

In my nine months in Villepinte, I came to better understand the mentality of kids from the projects. They reigned supreme. Because of them, visiting hours were longer and you could have meals together. If you forgot to buy something at the canteen, you didn't have to wait a week like in other prisons. They'd be friendly with the auxiliaries & you could get what you wanted inside an hour.

There was stuff that wasn't allowed, too. Inmates in ground-floor cells were in charge of collecting whatever was tossed into the prison from outside during the night. Hashish, or maybe a cell phone and charger, would be squirreled inside a soda can, wrapped in a little string bag, and pitched inside from a field alongside the highway. Despite security nets, they'd succeed in getting the packages in. Ground-floor inmates would then use a kind of stick elongated with string, at the end of which was attached a twisted fork that served as a hook. They'd cast these like fishermen and could pick up everything they wanted. I saw the most fantastic thing my very first night there. While watching TV, I heard a noise outside so I opened the window. Between the building to my left & the one facing it, I saw "funiculars"— at least fourteen strings along which packages were moving.

The young guys, for the most part, were friendly. Especially a group of blacks from Gagny. They'd got mixed up in credit card fraud. They were super-funny and spoke a kind of unimaginable slang from the projects. One of them, a young Algerian named Oueri, was the nephew of Abdenour, a big name in banditry.

Nordine la Gelée asked me for help when he arrived. He reminded me of myself two years earlier: he was dressed in jeans and Westons and seemed lost. I give him a couple of things — tracksuit, sneakers, and made him dinner. Talking to him made him feel much better, and he took me for an older brother. He became a good buddy. He was inside because of some affair with slot machines. He got out after a couple of months.

Later, I'd meet his cousin Malik: same as La Gelée, but stronger, and smart as a whip.

And then the sentencing ...

Yes. From Villepinte I was transferred to Amiens, where I was brought before criminal court. I got 20 years for the jewelry store in Chantilly, the bank robbery, and hostage-taking in Creil. But I was able to appeal. At the same time, I was found not guilty for an attack on the Brink's depot in Coudun, near Compiègne. I hadn't been involved.

After that, I was put on trial in Bobigny for armored truck robbery in Villepinte, and sentenced to 15 years. The prosecution had called for 25! At trial they asked me why I was known as "Doc." The prosecutor thought that it was because I operated with surgical precision. At the trial, I avoided mentioning Steve McQueen & said my nickname came from my life on the run, a nod to Richard Kimble in *The Fugitive*. In her summation, the prosecutor compared me to a cat that always lands on its feet. She pulled out all the stops and reminded the jury that I attacked an armored truck in front of a cash depot in Villepinte, which was located 600 feet from a police station and protected by 30 armed guards. She understood I did it to humiliate the guards and to ridicule the police. She noted that I loved using lines from the movie *Heat* in correspondence, that I was myself a character out of a Hollywood film. In short, she stuck it to me totally.

In the courtroom during the hearing, the armored truck guards waved to me. One of them would leave his address with my lawyer that I might write to him.

He'd found me to be decent: the Stockholm Syndrome is more powerful than you can imagine. With the BAC police, things also went well. They knew I'd no intention of shooting them; I even paid tribute to their courage. Cops from the BRB didn't say much because they didn't know me.

The judge recognized that I don't harbor hatred either toward society or the police. I was a thief, on the docket as a thief, & accepted responsibility.

During this time, were you still in prison in Villepinte?

No. For possession of a cell phone I'd been transferred to Bois-d'Arcy but kept there only six months. There I came across other members of the Dream Team. Also other young guys from the projects, but they were less friendly than those I'd known in the 93rd. But that didn't keep us from getting along.

From Bois-d'Arcy I was transferred to solitary at La Santé. There I met Christophe K., who'd attempted to escape from Fresnes by helicopter; Boualem B., a terrorist who'd set off explosives in the RER station at Saint-Michel; and Djamel, who'd escaped from Moulins Prison, also by helicopter. Among DPS prisoners, you found the mentality of the big-name gangsters from the 1980s and 1990s. You ran little risk of snitches.

How do you handle prison?

Time goes very, very, very slow... In solitary confinement, it's even slower. You spend your time reading and exercising. If you're lucky enough to be able to have family members visit, you're saved. The visitors' room is the medicine that relieves the pain of detention. I've met any number of guys in these fucking isolation units who don't have visitation rights.

The prison administration doesn't consider solitary confinement as a form of punishment, but that's exactly how the prisoner experiences it. I think that it's absolutely normal for such a prisoner to feel resentment. You don't get to see daylight, you can't talk with anybody. You get out for an hour in the morning and an hour in the afternoon, in a heavily fenced yard that looks like a basement. For the rest of the time, it's 22 hours a day in your cell. It's ultra-destructive, designed to break prisoners. As the guards are well aware. But they're not the ones who put you there. They escort you to the yard and keep an eye on you. With DPS prisoners, most are under pressure from their superiors. They become totally paranoid, which affects their judgment when you ask for the simplest things, like to take a shower, get out for a walk, or pass on something from the canteen to another inmate. Fortunately, they're not all like that. You have access to a gym, but you're always alone. And they tell you that this is not punishment. Sure, right — and by the way, it's all in your head. Seriously, though, you've got to have courage. Most guys you meet in isolation are DPS, in for armed robbery or, less frequently, terrorism.

In addition to being apart from your family, the penal administration transfers you every three months as part of the famous "security rotation." That's hard on both prisoners and families. In my view, it's the biggest injustice of the prison system. Families are really cut off, yet they're the ones who have to keep in touch with the lawyers, send mail and money for the canteen, and even do laundry. They form the prisoner's safety valve. The system should be delighted that prisoners receive visitors. They feel better afterwards. Visits help calm and pacify them and make life easier for the guards. Families must deal with terrible hardships when one of them is in jail. Visits require sacrifices because they're expensive and exhausting. It takes planning and maybe giving up a day's pay. How's it supposed to work if a family from Corsica must come to Paris to visit a prisoner? Plane, train, round-trip taxi, and then back home. Same problem for those from Lyon, Marseilles, Nantes. They destroy you in every way they can. Solitary confinement is not enough for them, so they try to shatter families. To keep all these guys away from them, in isolation, it's truly disgusting.

As you've told us, though, these guys have screwed up royally. So what do you expect?

When a guy commits a big crime, he's got to pay. Although most DPS prisoners that I met didn't have blood on their hands, that didn't stop the penal system from treating them like wild animals. Child rapists and killers — I never met a single one in QHS. As to the families, they did nothing wrong. Their only fault is to love the guy who's doing time; they had nothing to do with the crime. Children want to see their father. Same with the prisoner's wife, mother & father. So we have to stop talking bullshit. If you do time in a penitentiary 300 miles from home, it's going to be extremely difficult in the long term. And they know it perfectly well.

In the visitors' room, you come to know the inmates' families. These people show incredible love. It goes beyond fidelity, the family ties that bind, good friendship. It's genuine tenderness. I'm not a judge, it's true, but families deserve the right to be reunited once their loved ones are released from prison. For myself, let me just add that I never complained about all this with fellow prisoners, because I knew I was privileged. My own family never let me down. I owe them a great deal. I was truly lucky.

Would you recap your various convictions?

Because my appeal was to take place in Amiens, I was transferred from Santé to Douai. There I was acquitted for hostage-taking, so from 20 years my sentence was reduced to 12, which was fair. I didn't appeal.

So 12 in Amiens and 15 in Bobigny for the armored truck, plus six at Créteil for memory cards, & four in Senlis for my escape in Switzerland. In total: 37 years.

How did you take it?

What do you think?

You're definitively sentenced in 2003. Were you then transferred?

While I was in Douai, Antonio Ferrara made his escape from Fresnes.* Two days later, a prison van with 30 police officers came to get me. I'd never seen such a deployment. The van was guarded by three squad cars in front, three in back, and two motorcycle cops. Police were stationed at each toll booth to supervise passage...

I was transferred from Douai to Saint-Maur. I can tell you that a trip in a speeding police van when you're handcuffed in the back is hell. You understand why it's called a salad spinner. I spent the first few days at Saint-Maur in solitary confinement before being put in with the general population.

In a central penitentiary like that, the atmosphere is different. For example, one of the prisoners was Marcel Barbeault, a serial killer from the 1970s. His murders, which he always carried out at night or very early in the morning, earned him the nickname of "The Shadow Killer." He'd been in prison for 35 years. Other inmates had occupied the same cell for 16 years. When we arrived, I looked out my cell window and saw a garden with little narrow paths: it looked like a nursing home. People were out walking, going for their little daily stroll.

---

* A well-known figure in armed robbery in France, Ferrara's escape was made by helicopter & was front-page news in France in 2003.

Shit!!! I can't end up like this! It's a fucking hospice.

The warden and the supervisor were decent people. They made daily life for the inmates bearable. You can plays sports, there are televisions and refrigerators that work. They understood that guys with long sentences need acceptable living conditions. Even though there are watchtowers and reinforced walls, they let prisoners live their lives. They can even have conjugal visits.

There I met, among others, Karim T., an escape recidivist; Abdelkrim A., a well-known armed robber from Montreuil; Patrick M., a Parisian trafficker; Pierrot, an armed robber from Bordeaux; Pitou, a feuj gangster extradited from Israel for murder; Alain A., an accomplice to Pascal Payet in Grasse; Zidon S., of Vitry-sur-Seine; Saïd, who robbed ATMs and was a good soccer player. Not to forget François Besse or Jean-Claude Roman, the famous doctor who murdered his whole family; André R., who killed a guard during a jail break and got 20 years added to his sentence — a nice guy, smart, well-educated, easygoing, with whom I get along very well. They were all in for life, and for me to see them was a fucking shock.

Among 150 inmates, I was practically the youngest.

Without a reduced sentence, I'd have 37 years to do, and at this time I'd only done just five.

So how does it work out?

Six years in, I did something stupid. I got caught with a cell phone. The administration suspected me of planning an escape, and that led to my transfer to solitary confinement at Santé.

I arrived in the midst of the Ferrara hysteria: after his jail break, they decided to put all DPS prisoners in solitary confinement.

Only big names are there. I was there six or seven months. At the end of my stay, the administration finds a handwritten note hidden inside an exercise machine in the weight room. It referred to preparations underway for an escape attempt. We were subjected to a thorough search that led to the discovery of explosives in a shower stall. At the time, there were only four of us in solitary.

After the note was discovered, conditions become more severe. Guards wouldn't let us pass along food to each other, but we were able to hide things in the false bottom of water bottles that we brought with us when let out for a walk. I even managed to conceal little oriental pastries and hot tea. Mornings in the yard, I put my hand up to the fence and my Corsican co-detainee would touch my fingers to say hello. I succeeded in passing him a glass of tea and we shared the pastries. For a moment, we could make believe we were in Paris, drinking tea and looking at the stars... It was like a stolen touch of freedom.

Subsequently, I was transferred back to Fresnes, then to isolation in Nanterre, where the prisoners were young guys from the projects, holding up pretty well.

And after that, more transfers?

Yes, it's standard procedure, for security reasons, to keep prisoners from having time to dream up escape plans. That's why after Nanterre, I ended up in late 2006 in high security in Moulins, where I stayed almost three years. There the warden had grouped together all the psychopaths on one floor. We named it *Faites entrer l'accusé** because it held some seven of the prisoners whose stories were told on the TV series. So it was a kind of laboratory: Patrice Allègre, Guy George, Nadir Sedrati, Edgar Boulai. Every time we pass by, we hum the show's theme song. But we don't talk to these guys. The guards, on the other end, act friendly toward them. They were very dangerous on the outside but now inside, they're harmless — here, new victims aren't easy to find.

When it comes to release, how do prisoners prepare?

Many of them can't project themselves into the future because their date of release is too distant. Jail break? Today it's nearly impossible. A very few cling to that hope, it helps them cope, just as do others with sport or religion. Some don't even think about it because the very idea is too much for them. There's a cliché that says: "They've a good life inside because they're with their own." Whoever tells you that is a moron.

---

* "Bring on the Accused," a French television series that reconstructed crimes from the mid-20th century.

As for the crazies, there are a lot of them in prison, and they're in with the general population. You wonder why they're not cared for in a hospital setting. But hospitals are afraid to take them, so they end up in prison. It's a stupid mistake that someday is sure and certain to blow up in their faces.

Finally, some guys are lucky enough to have lawyers who try to free them from the nightmare. A lawyer has got to bust his guts to do it because the process is long and hard.

I'm lucky to have an absolutely wonderful lawyer. Jean-Louis Pelletier has never let me down. Never. I have to say, I've never given him a hard time. But each time I've written him, he's immediately come to visit. The guy is an angel. But I also get pissed at him a little because each time he speaks on my behalf, the cocksucker makes me cry. He's always telling me, "To succeed, we must work together. Otherwise, you've betrayed me." The prisoner must do his share: no discipline reports, join all the socio-cultural activities, undergo training that will help you find work after release, start to compensate the victims financially. Some among us start seeing a psychologist and work on themselves.

In solitary confinement, you can't do anything except stay in your cell. For that to change, you can only wait for sentencing and then transfer to a high-security penitentiary. And that can take years. But it's not easy because you're asked to change, and some prisoners think that means they have to disavow themselves totally. I can understand that, because you're mistreated so badly in prison... what with disciplinary cells, isolation, visitation difficulties, and repeated transfers. You get the impression that they have it in for you personally. You start to see every authority as the "enemy": psychologists, social workers, guards — everybody. Inmates need a lot of luck to encounter "good guys." Even if a prisoner with a long sentence shows good behavior and a willingness to rehabilitate, he's penalized by the crime he committed, what happens to his reputation, and his stature as DPS. It's truly deplorable. The parole adviser never meets with you because it's useless for him to learn more about you: he's read your report and already formed an opinion. He doesn't distinguish between the person and the crime. And in that case, you're as good as dead. You can only wait for the next transfer and hope to meet people who won't judge you a second time, as if they were magistrates!

And yet, you still must want to change. You must persevere and never give up. It's my family's love that makes me hold on and gives me the strength and the desire to succeed.

When you left QHS for the penitentiary, you started the process of rehabilitation. You obtained a sentence reduction.

Sentences for evading capture can't be reduced. When I got 15 years for the armored truck robbery at Villepinte, four extra years were added to my sentence for my escape in Switzerland. That makes a total of 19 years. It seems crazy but I was happy about it, considering time served. I've already spent nine years in jail, so now I can conceive of a future with "freedom."

This comes at the time you're transferred to the detention center in Meaux?

Exactly. After 9-½ years of high-security peniten-tiaries, I've ended up at this detention center, where I'm treated like a regular prisoner. With the sentence reduction I still have officially four more years. I'd already met the warden of this prison when I was in Villepinte in 2001. At the time she didn't want me there. She was afraid that some terrible rascals would come blow a hole in the wall to set me free. Which was false.

By the way, did you never plan an escape? Somebody like you would not be prepared to lose 10 years of his life in prison...

It's my turn to ask you a question. 250 inmates in a prison yard. Suddenly a hole opens in the wall. How many guys will rush toward the hole? What do you think?

Of course.

So you have your answer. Even guards, you know, find it normal that prisoners want to escape. It's a human reaction. "Freedom is not given," said Peter Kropotkin. "It's taken." In prison, I read books, too.

I want to come back to Meaux. You received permission for temporary furlough?

I had to show my genuine intention to leave prison by the front door. When I arrive at Meaux, I pressed the administration for authorization to work or enter a training program. I hate to be idle.

For a probatory period, they put me in a workshop with private assistants I got along with right away. They don't judge you. After a few weeks, they started to trust me and give me responsibilities. It seemed strange at first. Usually I exert authority over a different type of people. Here I had 30 prisoners depending on me. Most of them were foreigners, arrested for smuggling cocaine from South America. I try hard to make them understand the work we do. They call me "El Mago" — *The Magician*. It refers to my ability to get the day's work done and summon them back every morning. When I make the list for those who'll come to work the next day, I always favor the Chicanos, because they won't receive visits or money orders during the three or four years they'll spend in France.

I work from seven in the morning to four in the afternoon, with a break for lunch. After a day's work, I'm tired and it feels good. I don't smoke and never touch a cell phone. I avoid being known as a member of this or that group. I'm not lonely but try to stay as low-profile as possible. You have to steer clear of fights. The administration won't forgive anything. In my head, I'm ultra clean. I left behind all these guys in the penitentiary who had long stretches to finish. I tell myself that if this doesn't work for me, others won't follow in my footsteps. I want to break the cliché about prisoners in DPS. I know how to get along. I don't draw attention to myself.

Despite all this, my photo is the only one the supervisor keeps in his office, prominently placed atop a notebook that lists every move I make. They won't give up. But I accept that. After all, I'm not here for having stolen a crate of tomatoes. I can only hope they don't overdo it.

They're not over-zealous at Meaux. Detention here is another planet compared to a maximum-security penitentiary. The prisoners here all have short sentences. They're furloughed every two months, from one day to five days.

I was finally granted a furlough and as the day grew near, paranoid as I am, I was afraid they'd cancel it at the last minute, that the warden would be afraid I won't come back. They take the risk. They "trust" me.

I left the center one November Sunday in 2008. *Fuck!* I can't believe it. After almost 10 years! The air I breathe is not the same. All the colors of freedom knock me senseless. It's magical. Looking to the horizon, I can't believe it. My eyes burn. I see it all in Cinemascope. Words can't describe what I see or the way I feel. Nobody can imagine it. Freedom is too beautiful. It's priceless.

While on that first furlough, I get the idea to go swimming, to touch and feel the water. When I dive into the pool, it's like plunging from a waterfall into a lagoon. It's been ages since I've been in the water. I still know how to swim — it's wonderful. I recall all these people who made this moment possible. But I also think about all those who are still behind bars.

Returning when furlough ends, I'm sure I'll be greeted by fireworks and find the warden standing on a red carpet surrounded by cheerleaders and fireworks. A cocktail will be waiting to celebrate my return. I've spent my life running away... Coming back to ring the prison's front doorbell seems impossible. But of course, I did come back. There were no celebrations.

After that, you were released on conditional parole.

After several furloughs, I applied for parole. Because Jean-Louis Pelletier had retired, I went with the woman who'd been his associate. Her name is Rajae Izem. She's smart, astute, and subtle, a lawyer from a wealthy family. I realize that her parents had given her an excellent education. She trained with one of the most prestigious lawyers of the Paris bar. Jean-Louis Pelletier assured me that she's a regular prodigy. In addition to having grace and poise, she's a ferocious lawyer who knows her cases inside out. She makes an art of digging deep into the specifics of police reports. I go with her. I trust her and won't regret it.

To begin parole, I need an offer of employment. I get in touch with somebody I worked for once. He'd offered me a job while I was a student at the Jean

Rostand High School. He remembers me. I tell him everything about my current situation and my past. He agrees to hire me as a salesperson. He's in construction, an Algerian Jew who lives in Val-de-Marne. A self-taught businessman who's done well, a perfectionist without equal. I meet with him while on furlough and we got along well. Same thing with the other employees. But there's still a hitch with parole. I need a *carte d'identité*. I've always had false papers. My last *carte d'identité* was made in 1985 & it's gone.

While on furlough, in fact, I went to the police station to declare it lost, which must be done before requesting a new ID. Strange feeling, to enter a police station. In the past, I've only been taken there by car and brought through the back door. Handcuffed. That's the only way I ever entered a police station. I obtained the declaration I need but was in a hurry to get out of there. I swore never to lose my ID again! After that I went to city hall for the new *carte d'identité* in the name of *Rédoine Faïd*. Unbelievable! Papers under my real name. I've changed, obviously. Now when people call me Rédoine, I jump. In the past, I had to beg people to not use my name under any circumstance.

The best was yet to come. I had to go to a bank to open an account. At this point, I flipped out. What a mess... I go inside, white as a sheet. I almost can't breathe. It ends up going very well. They even give me a Visa card. No more cash, no more getaways. No more checking to see if I'm being followed. No more hiding from early afternoon to the next day.

The incredible stress at airports, the constant fear of the police. Living with death. Wondering if I'll still be alive tomorrow.

It's over. I'm a fucking legit!

We've often referred to movies. The cinema, for you as for other young men in the projects, occupies an important place in life. So in conclusion, I'd like you to tell me more about the little nod that destiny made in your direction after you were set free.

In June 2009, I met Michael Mann, who was in Paris for his new film, *Public Enemies*. Johnny Depp plays the role of John Dillinger, the ultra-famous American bank robber. Invited to the preview by the director of the Cinémathèque française, I had the pleasure of talking with someone whose work had influenced my life for some 20 years. I told him that he'd been both my best university professor and technical advisor. He laughed. My friends and I had viewed his films as semi-documentaries that told you what to do or not do: never squeal, use drugs, or shed blood, and stay away from big underworld gangsters. It's simple — ban the cinema and you'll reduce crime by 50 percent. Without making him feel guilty, I explained how his movies were an inspiration for young people. He was a little embarrassed. At the same time, he knows that *Heat*, a movie we watched together, is the best depiction of the world of police & armed robbery.

And now, are you happy?

I'm very happy. The pleasure you get from money and robbery at gunpoint is short-lived. For me, the most beautiful adventure hasn't ended. It's only suffered a setback.

POSTFACE

Two years after his early release from prison & the initial publication of *Braqueur*, Rédoine Faïd made headlines again. On January 11, 2011, he managed to evade a police raid on his home and disappeared. At the time he was under suspicion of having participated in planning a 2010 armored truck robbery that ended in the death of Aurélie Fouquet, a young policewoman, in Villiers-sur-Marne. While at large, Faïd proclaimed his innocence before he was arrested on June 28, 2011 in the north in Villeneuve d'Asq. Police from Lille came upon him by accident in a sandwich shop while they were surveilling suspects, connected with another similar robbery, with whom he was about to meet. His arrest put an end to a flight from justice that had made Faïd "public enemy number one" in France.

Less than two years later, Faïd escaped prison at Lille-Sequedin in northern France. On a Saturday morning in April 2013, while ostensibly making his way to the visiting area, he suddenly brandished an automatic revolver, took four guards hostage, and used explosives to blow open the prison doors. Once outside, he liberated the guards and fled in a waiting car driven by an accomplice. He was bearded and disguised when, some six weeks later, a little after 2:00 AM, police from one of the French anti-gang units arrested him in his hotel bed in Pontault-Combault, southeast of Paris.

Returned to prison yet again, he now underwent a long series of trials. For the 2010 robbery in Villiers-sur-Marne, he was convicted and sentenced, after appeals were exhausted, to 25 years for criminal conspiracy, in which the prosecution characterized him as mastermind of that lethal "coup." His 2013 escape from Lille-Sequedin added 10 years to his sentence in a trial that only concluded in 2017, and which he appealed. That year, he was also tried for participating in an armed robbery near Arras in March 2011, while he was at large. In that attack, false signage was used to misdirect highway traffic while a dump truck rammed and immobilized an armored truck and blasted it open using explosives — the thieves then extracted some 2,000,000 euros. Faïd's conviction for that crime brought a sentence of 18 years.

However, the most spectacular and unbelievable event was yet to come. In July 2018, Faïd escaped once again, this time from the central penitentiary at Réau, a banlieue southeast of Paris. A helicopter, whose pilot was taken hostage by three accomplices, set down in a prison courtyard that had no overhead security net. Two masked men armed with Kalashnikovs jumped out. They barged into the visitor's center at a time when Rédoine was there with one of his brothers. They used smoke bombs to blind the surveillance cameras and a power saw to cut through the bars. Within minutes, Faïd escaped in the company of the masked commandos, disappearing into the air. Days later, police discovered the burned-out getaway car that was used as a relay after the helicopter set down in a field north of Paris, following a tip from a hunter who had seen men bury a sack that turned out to contain the weapons used during the escape.

On July 24, after three weeks on the run, Faïd was spotted near Sarcelles, not far from Paris, after his vehicle drew the attention of police. He led gendarmes on a dramatic car chase but escaped. Subsequently, his car was discovered abandoned in the underground parking garage of a shopping center. Six sticks of fake plastic explosives were found in the trunk. But no Rédoine Faïd.

He remained on the loose for three more months, even as he became the most sought-after criminal in France. Faïd was arrested at 4:00 AM on October 3, 2018, in an apartment in Creil, the city where he was born, in the company of one of his brothers.

— Jérôme Pierrat

COLOPHON

OUTLAW: AUTHOR ARMED & DANGEROUS
was handset in InDesign CC.

The text font is *ParaType Serif & Sans*
The display font is *Breakout*.

Book design & typesetting: Alessandro Segalini
Cover image: Jean-Luc Bertini
Cover design: Alessandro Segalini & CMP

OUTLAW: AUTHOR ARMED & DANGEROUS
is published by Contra Mundum Press.

Contra Mundum Press   New York · London · Melbourne

CONTRA MUNDUM PRESS

Dedicated to the value & the indispensable importance of the individual voice, to works that test the boundaries of thought & experience.

The primary aim of Contra Mundum is to publish translations of writers who in their use of form and style are *à rebours*, or who deviate significantly from more programmatic & spurious forms of experimentation. Such writing attests to the volatile nature of modernism. Our preference is for works that have not yet been translated into English, are out of print, or are poorly translated, for writers whose thinking & æsthetics are in opposition to timely or mainstream currents of thought, value systems, or moralities. We also reprint obscure and out-of-print works we consider significant but which have been forgotten, neglected, or overshadowed.

There are many works of fundamental significance to *Weltliteratur* (& *Weltkultur*) that still remain in relative oblivion, works that alter and disrupt standard circuits of thought — these warrant being encountered by the world at large. It is our aim to render them more visible.

For the complete list of forthcoming publications, please visit our website. To be added to our mailing list, send your name and email address to: info@contramundum.net

Contra Mundum Press
P.O. Box 1326
New York, NY 10276
USA

OTHER CONTRA MUNDUM PRESS TITLES

2016   Jean-Luc Godard, *Phrases*
        Otto Dix, *Letters, Vol. 1*
        Maura Del Serra, *Ladder of Oaths*
        Pierre Senges, *The Major Refutation*
        Charles Baudelaire, *My Heart Laid Bare & Other Texts*
2017   Joseph Kessel, *Army of Shadows*
        Rainer J. Hanshe & Federico Gori, *Shattering the Muses*
        Gérard Depardieu, *Innocent*
        Claude Mouchard, *Entangled — Papers! — Notes*
2018   Miklós Szentkuthy, *Black Renaissance*
        Adonis & Pierre Joris, *Conversations in the Pyrenees*
2019   Charles Baudelaire, *Belgium Stripped Bare*
        Robert Musil, *Unions*
        Iceberg Slim, *Night Train to Sugar Hill*
        Marquis de Sade, *Aline & Valcour*
2020   *A City Full of Voices: Essays on the Work of Robert Kelly*

SOME FORTHCOMING TITLES

        Carmelo Bene, *I Appeared to the Madonna*
        Paul Celan, *Microliths They Are, Little Stones*

THE FUTURE OF KULCHUR
A PATRONAGE PROJECT

With bookstores and presses around the world struggling to survive, and many actually closing, we are forming this patronage project as a means for establishing a continuous & stable foundation to safeguard our longevity. Through this patronage project we would be able to remain free of having to rely upon government support &/or other official funding bodies, not to speak of their timelines & impositions. It would also free CMP from suffering the vagaries of the publishing industry, as well as the risk of submitting to commercial pressures in order to persist, thereby potentially compromising the integrity of our catalog.

CAN YOU SACRIFICE $10 A WEEK FOR KULCHUR?

For the equivalent of merely 2–3 coffees a week, you can help sustain CMP and contribute to the future of kulchur. To participate in our patronage program we are asking individuals to donate $500 per year, which amounts to $42/month, or $10/week. Larger donations are of course welcome and beneficial. All donations are tax-deductible through our fiscal sponsor Fractured Atlas. If preferred, donations can be made in two installments. We are seeking a minimum of 300 patrons per year and would like for them to commit to giving the above amount for a period of three years.

WHAT WE OFFER

Part tax-deductible donation, part exchange, for your contribution you will receive every CMP book published during the patronage period as well as 20 books from our back catalog. When possible, signed or limited editions of books will be offered as well.

WHAT WILL CMP DO WITH YOUR CONTRIBUTIONS?

Your contribution will help with basic general operating expenses, yearly production expenses (book printing, warehouse & catalog fees, etc.), advertising & outreach, and editorial, proofreading, translation, typography, design and copyright fees. Funds may also be used for participating in book fairs and staging events. Additionally, we hope to rebuild the *Hyperion* section of the website in order to modernize it.

From Pericles to Mæcenas & the Renaissance patrons, it is the magnanimity of such individuals that have helped the arts to flourish. Be a part of helping your kulchur flourish; be a part of history.

HOW

To lend your support & become a patron, please visit the subscription page of our website: contramundum.net/subscription

For any questions, write us at: info@contramundum.net

CPSIA information can be obtained
at www.ICGtesting.com
Printed in the USA
LVHW052015010422
715081LV00004B/212